SAGE COURSE COMPANIONS
KNOWLEDGE AND SKILLS *for* SUCCESS

Criminology

James Treadwell

SAGE Publications

London • Thousand Oaks • New Delhi

First published 2006

Apart from any fair dealing for the purposes of research
or private study, or criticism or review, as permitted
under the Copyright, Designs and Patents Act, 1988, this
publication may be reproduced, stored or transmitted in
any form, or by any means, only with the prior
permission in writing of the publishers, or in the case of
reprographic reproduction, in accordance with the terms
of licences issued by the Copyright Licensing Agency.
Enquiries concerning reproduction outside those terms
should be sent to the publishers.

 SAGE Publications Ltd
1 Oliver's Yard
55 City Road
London EC1Y 1SP

SAGE Publications Inc.
2455 Teller Road
Thousand Oaks, California 91320

SAGE Publications India Pvt Ltd
B-42, Panchsheel Enclave
Post Box 4109
New Delhi 110 017

British Library Cataloguing in Publication data

A catalogue record for this book is available from
the British Library

ISBN 1 4129 1133 8   ISBN 13 978 1 4129 1133 7
ISBN 1 4129 1134 6   ISBN 13 978 1 4129 1134 4

Library of Congress Control Number available

Typeset by C&M Digitals (P) Ltd., Chennai, India
Printed on paper from sustainable resources
Printed in Great Britain by The Cromwell Press, Trowbridge, Wiltshire

contents	

Part One   Introduction to Your Course Companion   1

1.1   Introduction   2
1.2   How to use this book   2
1.3   Why use this book?   3
1.4   Criminology basics: Thinking like a criminologist   5
1.5   What is crime?   6
1.6   Perspectives on crime   8
1.7   Categorising criminological theory   12

Part Two   Core Areas of the Curriculum   13

Running themes in criminology   14

2.1   The origins of criminology   16
2.2   Research methods in criminology   24
2.3   Locating crime within the individual: Biological
       and psychological approaches   33
2.4   Crime as external to the individual:
       Sociological theories   42
2.5   Contemporary criminology   55
2.6   Crime statistics and crime data   66
2.7   Crime and the media   75
2.8   Youth and crime   84
2.9   Gender and crime   91
2.10   Penology   98
2.11   Serious crime   108
2.12   Victimology   117

Part Three   Study, Writing and Revision Skills
               (in collaboration with David McIlroy)   **127**

3.1   General introduction   128
3.2   Dealing with theory   129
3.3   How to get the most out of your lectures   132

3.4   How to get the most out of your seminars   136
3.5   Essay writing tips   140
3.6   Revision hints and tips   149
3.7   Exam tips   155

Part Four   Additional Resources   **169**

Glossary of key terms and criminologists   170

Bibliography   182

Index   190

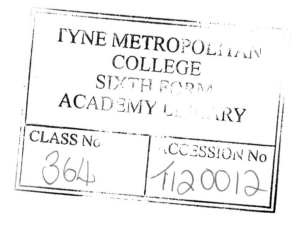

For Abi and my family

part one
introduction to your course companion

Core areas: 1.1 **Introduction**

1.2 **How to use this book**

1.3 **Why use this book?**

1.4 **Criminology basics:**
    Thinking like a criminologist

1.5 **What is crime?**

1.6 **Perspectives on crime**

1.7 **Categorising criminological theory**

1.1

introduction

When I first encountered criminology, I was keen to know more about what the subject involved. My introduction to criminology came in the form of a fairly complicated textbook I purchased before the first term of my degree that had been recommended by a tutor. As I tried to comprehend what was contained within its pages, I found myself gripped by a strange feeling of dread. I had never counted myself amongst the most successful students and can acknowledge now, with perhaps less shame than I felt then, that I struggled to understand the subject. Persistence clearly paid off, but I can empathise with the difficulties that those new to this field might encounter.

This book seeks to assist those new to the discipline who are unsure of the subject and who are looking to understand the basics of criminology. It is not intended to replace textbooks, journals and more specialist texts. It aims to make the initial stages of the journey in studying criminology a little less complex, introducing the theories and terms that are common to criminology. If those new to the discipline can make use of this book in the initial stages of study then it has served its purpose well.

1.2

how to use this book

The key to success in any criminology course is not to simply learn and use academic language. Nor is it simply to understand 'core' theories, although knowing the terms and concepts that mark out 'academic criminology' from everyday debates about crime and criminal justice is certainly part of the journey. This book will give you hints and tips about how to understand and use criminological theory, and how to apply and critique this theory when you encounter debates upon crime, criminality and the criminal justice system.

This book has been designed firstly as an introduction. Thereafter it will provide you with a guide that you can use as a reference point (to works that you should then read yourself). You should use Part 2 of this book to give you an overview of topic areas that you are likely to encounter, and build on what you find. You can always use the 'Taking it further' section and the Textbook guide to explore the subject in more detail, and you should also note the theorists mentioned in the book and attempt to read some of their work. Although there are summaries of the works of leading criminologists in textbooks, nothing can replace the knowledge that you will gain from making yourself familiar with the original works.

To that end you should not simply passively read the references here, but make use of them. In the first instance, having read a chapter you should turn to the Textbook guide which will direct you to further reading. However, after this you should use the references in the text, and use these to inform your reading. When you find references in the text you can trace these to the Bibliography at the back of the book. Once you have the full reference for a book that you think will be useful to you try to trace the text. You can do this in several ways: The first stop should be your university library, but you can also use the internet and local bookstores to try and find a text. It is important that you do not come to rely upon one book, but instead learn how to direct your reading to other relevant sources and material.

1.3	
why use this book?	

This book is also intended to help you to monitor your progress as you develop in your study. Progress will be made through reading and gaining insight, but it is also likely that you will have to prove your knowledge, and often this will require that you produce some form of written assessment. For that reason this book also contains a sample question in each chapter, although this is not intended as a template that will guarantee exam success. You can always use these as practice for the real thing; and practice will make you better.

The most unique feature of this book is that it contains two sections (Parts 2 and 3) that complement and support one another and, if used in conjunction should assist you in becoming a more informed and competent student. Part 2 of this book provides an examination of 'over-arching' criminological theories (that is, those theories that inform 'academic' criminology and that criminologists use to support the arguments that they make) which are combined with more general discussions in the field. It is hoped that encountering both the theory and practice of academic criminology will help you to develop a more comprehensive knowledge of the subject. I will re-state the point here that academic criminology and the theory that we use is never separate from what happens in the 'real world' of practice, and students should know not only about theory, but practices in 'the real world' of crime and the criminal justice system.

Part 3 of this book has been designed to assist you in developing and sharpening the study skills that are necessary for studying criminology and is best used in conjunction with Part 2. It is intended to assist you in developing your skills so that you get the best from your reading, and it will assist you in developing a range of skills. However, these skills and your ability will only be fully rounded if you combine them with the academic knowledge and understanding that come from engaging and practicing criminology, and therefore the aim is for Parts 2 and 3 to support each other and be used in conjunction.

A final unique feature of this book is the incorporation of Tips and Common pitfalls. When reading criminology it is best that you adopt a questioning mind. Do not simply accept what you are told but always ask the question 'Why?'. The Tips and Common pitfalls are intended to highlight areas for you to consider, sometimes giving practical advice or making an important point, or raising a question for you to reflect upon. Common pitfalls contain some common mistakes or misunder-standings that exist in the discipline. These features are intended to stimulate you and cause you to question the assertions and arguments that criminologists make; and therefore to help you develop 'critical thinking'. With that point in mind it is worth reiterating that it is not just the essential study skills and theoretical knowledge that are required to pass a criminology course, your hard work is undeniably the most important component.

part two

core areas of the curriculum

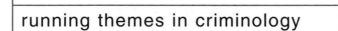

running themes in criminology

Throughout this book, the reader will be asked to consider running themes. These are some of the issues and considerations that underpin the discipline of criminology, and have to be considered regardless of the topic. The reader is encouraged to re-visit the running themes continually, and reflect upon the subject matter with these themes in mind, asking questions about how each theme may impact upon individual subject areas.

Running themes

No matter what area of criminology you are writing about, it is important that you try, wherever possible, to mention these themes and think about how they make an impact upon the subject:

- **Inequality** – Who loses and who gains in a social context? Is something fair, and are people regarded equally? If not there may be inequality
- **Power** – Who defines the agenda, and how do they use force, ideas, language etc. to control behaviour?
- **Evidence** – How convincing is an argument? What basis does the argument have? Little is ever proven, and there will be a counter argument
- **Class** – How does our social background affect our opportunities, our choices, and our identity?
- **Discrimination** – Is one group, or groups disproportionately advantaged or disadvantaged? Are some people being treated markedly differently to the advantage or disadvantage of others?
- **Sex and gender** – How does being male or female differ in a given social context, and how does the social context shape our options as women or as men?
- **Race** – How does ethnicity make a difference? Some people may face prejudice and inequality because of their ethnicity and culture
- **Research methods** – How have the methods used to generate social observations made those observations any more or any less convincing to you? You should also consider what the research is based upon. Is the research based upon evidence, and what is the evidence? How does the research base support any claims being made?

- **Age** – Whether you are old or young, a child or a grown-up, you will experience social life differently and may have different opportunities
- **Ideology** – What are the tacit rules and regulations that govern how we think about every social problem, and what is it that stops us thinking differently?
- **Politics/economics** – How do either the politics and/or economics of the issue limit choice and govern social action?
- **Application** – Theories may have a practical purpose. What are, or might be the practical implications of a theory?
- **Representation** – What picture is being portrayed? What is being suggested, and by what/who?
- **Justice** – This has a variety of applications, but most literally could be taken as incorporating the notion of fairness and appropriateness in the exercise of authority. Is a concept fair, does it treat the subject appropriately? This however is a subjective concept. It is not fixed or universal, but based upon individual opinion and judgement.

Using running themes

When writing about crime you will need to talk about how crime is not a simple concept. You could argue that crime is not something we can all define and may argue that who defines crime is a matter of power. You could suggest that crime reflects inequality in terms of those who experience it – the experience of crime (and the perpetration of crime) differs according to whether you are working class or middle class, male or female, black or white, young or old. You will also need to remember, as is suggested below, that the nature and experience of crime is always changing, as are the methods we use to both record it and control it. Already, in a short space of time you have begun to inter-weave some of the running themes listed above. Without naming a particular study or theorist, you have already set out a strong structure to any argument, and you are showing that you can think like a criminologist.

2.1

the origins of criminology

Core areas: **The contested origins of criminology**
Spiritual explanations
A capital system
The background to the development of criminology
Cesare Beccaria – The philanthropist?
Beccaria – *On Crimes and Punishments*
Criticisms of classicism

Running themes

Classical criminology was based on arguments about the cause of crime and how it should be dealt with. It had no concern with **research methods** as it was not based upon **evidence**, but instead on arguments about the **ideology** of crime and punishment. Therefore, classical criminology is inspired by **political** and **economic** thought. That stated, the motivations that influenced this school of criminology are not clear. Some criminologists would argue that classicism served to challenge **inequality** and inappropriate use of **power**, while others feel that it is **class** biased, and its central motivation was to continue to promote **inequalities** and the authority and **power** of the social elite.

Key thinkers

Cesare Beccaria (1738–94)   Cesare Bonesana, Marchese de Beccaria (more frequently referred to as Cesare Beccaria) was born to a respected aristocratic family in Milan, Italy. Cesare Beccaria was a philosopher with an interest in economics. Through a friendship with Alessandro Verri (who was at the time the Protector for Prisoners) he was persuaded to write on the topic of crime and punishment. Initially publishing his work *Dei Deliti e Delle Penne* (*On Crimes and Punishments*) in 1764 anonymously through fear as to how it would be received. His fear was ill founded and Beccaria eventually came to be much respected.

Jeremy Bentham (1748–1832)   Bentham was a British Jurist and philosopher who is associated with the concept of utilitarianism, but his contribution to criminology is varied and includes the design of the Panopticon prison, a model that was to influence much Victorian prison building.

The contested origins of criminology

The origins of criminology as an academic discipline are contested, but most criminology courses and textbooks will begin by examining the contribution of a school of thought called 'classicism' or 'classical criminology'. This is by no means universally accepted as the origin of criminology, because for some criminologists it is not possible to regard what was essentially a philosophical strand of thought as the origin of criminology.

It is also worth stressing at this point that Classicism may be a concept that is perhaps used more for academic's convenience than because of the existence of a unified 'classical school' of criminology. In creating a category of classical criminology, textbook histories often conform to one of two styles: The first style highlights one or two prominent names giving rise to the false idea that these stand out as isolated contributors. The second convention paints a no more accurate picture, and tends to bring together a range of contributors to early criminology that could only be linked very tenuously.

Part of the problem is that there does not exist an identifiable starting point for criminology as a subject; it is not possible to find a logical or decisive moment in which 'criminology' was created (in just the same way as it is not possible to suggest a universal rule that explains all crime). There is a great deal of merit in studying early contributions to debates about the causation of crime, because if you can understand this background, you are probably better placed to understand contemporary criminology.

Spiritual explanations

Spiritual explanations for crime form part of a general view of life in which events are linked to a higher power, or the influence of otherworldly powers.

Primitive people believed natural events such as earthquakes, famines and floods were punishments sent by spiritual powers or gods (divine retribution) to punish wrong-doing. In the middle ages this spirituality became linked to political systems; with society structured around monarchy and aristocracy creating feudal systems to which we can trace the origins of our criminal justice system. In these systems, crime was often avenged or dealt with between family groups and allegiance, or by those with power. Taking blood oaths of vengeance by victims was common, and the principals regarding punishment often involved exacting justice by revisiting harm proportionate or greater than that done initially, back upon the offender (eye for an eye).

Feudal justice systems were based upon rights of power whereby 'God's will' would see justice done. Examples of this are trial by battle whereby two opposing parties (or their representatives) would fight in combat with God giving victory to the winner; the loser, having no grounds for attempting to exact revenge. Trial by ordeal was introduced somewhat later (an example being trial by fire where holding or walking on burning coals was used to determine guilt). In western European systems the link between law and monarchy was one that continued in most countries until modern times. That said, the method for punishing wrong-doing was often crude, and progressed little from cruel vengeance.

A capital system

From the fifth century in Anglo-Saxon England when execution by 'hanging' emerged as the dominant form of punishment for many offences (it was applied with alarming frequency until around the end of the 1850s), the methods for delivering punishment were often cruel and gruesome. In England, women charged with 'petty treason' (killing their spouse) were covered in tar and burnt at the stake in public until 1789. Punishments often made little allowances for mitigation. In 1708, Michael Hammond (then aged 7) and his sister (aged 11) were reputedly hanged for felony offences, if true, Michael would have been the youngest person ever to suffer the death penalty in Britain. Even in the nineteenth century capital punishment was a sentence that was applicable to a vast range of crimes (in 1822 English and Welsh law listed a staggering 222 capital criminal offences). Gradually the use of transportation to America (and later Australia) allowed for death sentences to be commuted to transportation, and there was a shift in the nature of punishment from corporal punishment to imprisonment (Foucault, 1977). However, it is largely execution and savage retribution and injustice that form the backdrop to the emergence of classical criminology. Even with the Penitentiary Act, the first English legislation authorising state run prisons passed in 1779, punishment was often a violent and painful experience.

The background to the development of criminology

The majority of criminological textbooks tend to begin their accounts in the mid-eighteenth century. Indeed it is easy to see why criminology's origins are linked to this time. Britain provides illustration of the way writings on the subject of law, crime and criminals became increasingly visible.

In 1756, William Blackstone published his lectures; a conservative appraisal of 'the *Development of the Laws of England*' suggested that the development of the law embodied the collective wisdom of society. It was in criticism of this notion that Bentham published a critical response and set the foundations for the principals of unity (and the concept of utilitarianism) in 1776. Utiliatrianism is a concept that is often associated with classical criminology.

Utilitarianism

As a concept utilitarianism stems from the work of Jeremy Bentham and John Stuart Mill. It is a moral theory that asserts that what is good is that which seeks to minimise pain, but maximise pleasure. The other core principal of utilitarianism is that the aim of good law should be to promote the greatest happiness for the greatest number.

Cesare Beccaria – The philanthropist?

Many books on criminology will link the origins of criminology to Cesare Beccaria. As an Italian aristocrat, Beccaria was able to turn his attention to philosophical debates on crime. It has to be remembered that the society in which Beccaria existed was far different to that which exists today. Western European states were largely governed by monarchy, with the monarch and the state assuming moral responsibility to impose punishment on offenders (in effect, assuming the authority of God and claiming a divine power to impose punishment on offenders).

These punishments, as illustrated above, were often cruel and harsh, based upon the infliction of pain and suffering. Many countries used the death penalty excessively for a wide range of offences. With severe and barbaric punishments commonplace, torture rife, and capricious judges interpreting the law often on whim (or adding punishments for personal reasons), the system of law was perhaps rife for reform. A number of criminological textbooks will regard 'classicism' as an example of enlightened humanitarian thinking. Beccaria's work is often regarded as an example of 'enlightenment' thinking that emerged in the late eighteenth century as a challenge to the dominance of spiritual and religious ideas.

Of course an alternative view exists, which suggests that the increasing concern with the welfare of offenders must be considered in the context of a more general shift in western European states. These societies were beginning to move towards an industrial phase, the ruling class could ill afford to damage or destroy the bodies of the labouring classes any longer. For that reason, it has been suggested that punishment of the body was being replaced by 'control' over it (a concept that stems from the seminal work of Michael Foucault, 1977).

The concern of the ruling classes about their privilege and its potential to be challenged might also provide a motivation for classicism. It is worth noting that when Beccaria published *On Crimes and Punishments* in 1764, the world was entering a period characterised by challenges to monarchy and the authority of states. The American Revolution occurred only just over a decade later (in 1776), followed by the French revolution (in 1789). Both displayed a lack of will to accept as given the power of rulers, which would have concerned the social elite throughout Europe. Therefore any analysis of 'classicism' or classical criminology should consider the perceived threat to the power of the dominant class and how this might have served to motivate them to create more humane regimes, rather than regard the motivation simply with a humane concern for promoting justice.

Beccaria – *On Crimes and Punishments*

On Crimes and Punishments was essentially a challenge to the Italian state's existing criminal justice systems. Beccaria protested against the inconsistencies in government and the management of public affairs. A particular point of contention for him was what he perceived to be purely personal justice that was being administered by judges.

Beccaria's arguments are well documented, however they are essentially philosophical rather than based upon research evidence, and were clearly based upon value judgements that he made.

Cesare Beccaria's *On Crimes and Punishments* (1764)

- Men give up, or sacrifice a proportion of their liberty so as to enjoy the rest of it in peace and security. The sum of those portions is what makes up the sovereignty of a nation
- But this alone is not enough, because these portions must be defended against individuals who may attempt to usurp a greater share. Some people will try not only to withdraw *their* share, but that of others. Tangible motives are needed to prevent this, and these motives are punishments established against those who may break the law
- The despotic spirit and the propensity to commit crime exists within all people
- Punishment should be dictated by legislation, and not decided by the courts
- Punishment that exceeds that limit fixed in law is not just punishment. The law should set punishments, and it should not be possible for judges to go beyond the limits set in law
- The true measure of crime is not the harm done to society, but the harm the criminal intended to do
- There must be a proper proportion between crimes and punishments (the punishment should fit the crime)
- Punishment is effective when the damage that it does exceeds the advantage gained from the crime
- The more promptly the punishment follows the crime, the more just and useful it is
- One of the most effective curbs on crimes is not the severity of the punishment, but the certainty that punishment will follow crime
- The laws must be clear and simple, so everyone may understand them
- Activities not expressly prohibited by law are permissible
- As punishment was to be imposed for deterrence, capital punishment for the most part should be abolished
- Classicism formed the basis for the French penal Code of 1791, and some of the core principles of classicism can still be seen in the administration of justice to this day.

Criticisms of classicism

There are problems with the classical position, for example, the assumption of freewill could be argued to be flawed. The idea that criminals are fundamentally rational and offend due to a desire for pleasure is one that will never gain universal acceptance. Such views tend to regard those who offend as having a choice, but there are other reasons that people offend, and not all people have the same options or choices available to them. This view takes little of the inequality of opportunities in society into consideration, which is perhaps unsurprising when one considers the background of those who generated it.

- Classicism assumes that people weigh up the costs and benefits of their crimes before they commit them, this may be true for some criminals, but it is not the case for all. We know that many crimes are spontaneous and ill considered
- Classicism assumed that people are knowledgeable about the punishments for crimes but again, this is often not the case, as many people do not know what the punishment for a specific offence is
- Classicism made argument for treating all people as alike – therefore the first-time offender commits an act as grave as the serial recidivist, the young and the mentally ill are equally culpable, first-time offenders are treated in the same way as repeat offenders
- The idea that everyone suffers the same punishment in the same way may be naïve. People have different responses to punishment. We know that for some offenders prison is a terrible experience, while others might suggest that they find it comforting and familiar
- Judging seriousness of a crime on the basis of act alone, and not intention, is also problematic. This view would see a 'cold blooded' and premeditated murder the same as an accidental or involuntary homicide. The harm resultant is the same; someone dies; yet the intent is markedly different. Classicism suggests no distinction need be made
- Classicism advocates a universal acceptance of the law simply because it is law, and does not question whether such laws are fair or just. It does not take into account the fact that societies are inherently unfair. For some people the cost of adhering to the social contract is nothing, and yet they gain a great deal of protection (especially those who are privileged and have a lot to lose). For others the costs are great and the benefits few. If we accept that this is the case, then increasing the benefits of adhering to the social contract may be more effective than having punishment for those who breach it. This however was not an attractive option to some social contract theorists who tended to come from a status group within society.

If you want to write about classicism, you would be well advised to consider the 'Running themes' such as those of inequality, power and class. How does classicism acknowledge these issues? Also, what is its research base and research methodology? How effective and useful would you evaluate classicism as being? Consider this using the Running themes and criteria for evaluating theory given in Chapter 3.2.

"What were the factors that influenced the development of classical criminology?"

Too many students fail to adequately address the fact that there are a wide range of criminologists that can be associated with the classical tradition and fail to make this point. A good answer will identify some of the features of classical criminology, and make a well-rounded argument about its development. Remember that there are two perspectives you can take; one holds that classicism was inspired by humanitarian concerns, the other that it was the product of a ruling class keen to protect its property. You should try to decide which you feel is more convincing and why. Remember to mention some specific theorists and their works.

Taking it ***FURTHER***

I would encourage students to develop a more insightful view of the origins of criminology than most textbooks provide, and therefore suggest that Newman and Marongiu, Young and Bernie's insightful chapters on classicism are essential reading; all of which can be found in a collection edited by Piers Beirne (1994) *The Origins and Growth of Criminology*.

Textbook guide

Exerts of both Beccaria and Bentham's works appear in McLaughlin et al., (2003) *Criminological Perspectives*. At the beginning of any criminology course I would encourage students to purchase a copy of *The Sage Dictionary of Criminology* (McLaughlin and Muncie, 2001) which may prove difficult reading at first, but ultimately is an invaluable resource. Understanding criminology without a working knowledge of the criminal justice system and its processes would be an extremely difficult endeavour, and therefore I also recommend *The Student Handbook of Criminal Justice and Criminology* (Muncie and Wilson, 2004) to students new to the discipline.

2.2

research methods in criminology

Core areas: **Research in criminology**

Primary and secondary research

Quantitative research methods

Qualitative research methods

Combined methods

Epistemology: Positivist, interpretivist and critical

Ethics

Access

The politics of criminological research

 Running themes

Questions about research and its **evidence** base will underpin almost all considerations of criminological theory. What is it that leads a criminologist to his/her
conclusions; what do they base their assertions on? In many cases research in
criminology will be based upon empirical work, and therefore we need to understand and ask questions about the **research methods** being used if we are to
determine whether the picture being presented is a fair **representation**. It should
be remembered that the research process is one that involves **power**, and can
be influenced by eternal factors such as **politics** and **economics**.

Research in criminology

In order to develop an understanding of criminology it is vital that
you have some knowledge about the practice of generating 'empirical'
research on crime and criminal justice. Criminologists seek to prove or
support theories with evidence; often relying upon empirical evidence

(which means evidence based upon observation and experiment and not just theory alone).

Not all criminological research is empirical, there is a wealth of criminological research that is purely 'theoretical', and this does not necessarily make that work invalid. In criminology the two have to co-exist, so empirical research is used to make theoretical arguments, or generate concepts that will become theories. Alternatively having a theory, idea or hypothesis may be the starting point for conducting empirical research.

> *As a criminologist it is important that you can comment on whether research is good or not, and in order to do this you have to be able to evaluate theories (this is covered in more detail in Part 3).*

> *By 'empirical' we mean that it is based upon knowledge that has been generated by observation and experiment, rather than simply upon theory.*

Primary and secondary research

As a social science, criminology has two types of data that may be used in research process. The first 'primary' data to the social scientist is data that they themselves have collected. A variety of different research methods may have been used to collect this data (for example interviews, questionnaires and observations). A 'secondary' source is information that has been produced by someone else, but a social scientist uses it for his or her own purposes.

Primary and secondary data

- **Primary Methods** – these involve data collection methods such as observation, questionnaires, structured and semi-structured interviews, focus groups, and participant observations
- **Secondary Methods** – these involve re-analysing official crime statistics and using existing literature, information obtained from previous research, or from someone else.

Quantitative research methods

Most criminologists need for theory to be supported by some form of 'empirical' evidence gained from research, and therefore will actively undertake research. When they do this they will tend to draw upon one tradition in research.

There are essentially two traditional research methods in criminological research, the first, what we call the quantitative tradition, emerged with the early positivists and moral statisticians, who proposed that it was possible to study society scientifically.

Researchers who adhere to a quantitative approach are concerned with explaining crime and predicting future patterns of criminal behaviour. Early positivists were keen to move away from simply philosophical discussions about crime and instead study society and social phenomena by drawing upon methods and ideas associated with the natural sciences. They were concerned with developing knowledge about the 'causation' of human behaviour, including criminal behaviour that could be presented in the form of rules or laws.

Clearly, if causes could be found, then so might cures, and therefore much early positivistic criminology (such as the work of Lombroso) was thought to be potentially useful. Often positivists start with a hypothesis (that is an idea or concept) that they will then seek to prove or disprove by testing, much like in the natural sciences.

Quantitative work continues to be undertaken in criminology, and much of the research that is produced by government departments is quantitative in nature. It is perhaps important to state here though that there has been a distinct shift in much quantitative work in criminology. The zealous search for a 'cause' of crime is no longer the driving force behind most criminology, and criminologists do not often seek to put forward a causal explanation for all crime. Quantitative researchers no longer conform to the narrow positivistic traditions that early criminologists did. Instead they tend to focus on a vast array of factors that may influence trends in crime or criminal behaviour.

Qualitative research methods

The second approach of undertaking criminological research is the qualitative approach. This approach was developed in the Chicago School of Sociology in the United States in the 1920s and 1930s. Much of the product of the Chicago School's research was concerned with the study of the sociology of deviance, and relied upon ethnographic methods.

Ethnography is the study of people and groups in their natural setting, typically involving the researcher spending prolonged periods of time systematically gathering data about their day to day activities, and the meanings that are attached to them.

Qualitative research rejects the notion that society and social phenomena can be studied in the same way as natural phenomena. Included in the Chicago School's ethnographies were studies of homelessness, prostitution and delinquent gangs. These theories gained followers and influence, where they continued to provide rich insight into the subculture of deviant groups (perhaps best known is Becker's 1963 study of cannabis use titled *Outsiders*). By the 1950s this approach had started to influence British sociologists producing studies of youth delinquency (Mays, 1954; Downes, 1966). More recently, qualitative research has been increasingly accepted by academics, and has been used to study a variety of topics in criminology. It has also been extremely influential upon those who now term themselves 'cultural criminologists'. It is generally accepted that qualitative research can offer rich insights into people's attitudes, beliefs and values and therefore is extremely useful to criminologists.

Combined methods

Whilst you could now be forgiven for believing that quantitative and qualitative methods are opposed, caution is advised and we must be mindful not to be drawn into thinking that the distinctions between the two are always immediately apparent. While it is true to suggest that some researchers divide the two methods (and themselves) into distinct camps from where they can be very critical of the opposition, many researchers tend to use methods combining quantitative and qualitative analysis, (sometimes in the same research study). This is done in order that they use a robust and defensible methodology, and to pre-empt and counter potential criticisms.

Epistemology

Social scientific researchers are not only influenced by research methods, but also by ideas about how knowledge is generated. To describe this we use the word 'epistemology', which literally means theories of knowledge. The term epistemology describes a researcher's beliefs about the nature of the social world that is under study, and assumptions made about how we should generate knowledge.

Regardless of the methods that researchers use, there are different 'epistemological' positions that they will occupy, that may (but will not necessarily) influence their selected research methods.

In criminology there exist different theories of knowledge, which we term 'epistemologies'. These flow from the early philosophical debates in the social sciences:

Positivist

The first epistemology is the 'positivist' epistemology, which is now widely considered amongst social scientists to be an outdated view.

Those that subscribe to a positivist epistemology believe that it is possible to be value-neutral when conducting research, and that by being value-neutral, the research is objective and not influenced by the researchers' own values or opinions. The main concern with this approach is the discovery of casual factors and relationships (for example, does a lack of street lighting cause a higher level of crime). As an approach it is often linked with quantitative research, generating a hypothesis or idea such as the previous example, which is then subjected to testing.

Interpretivist

The interpretivist approach rejects the concept that science and scientific method can be used to study the thoughts and feelings that impact upon human behaviour and interactions, and that the only way that researchers generate ideas is by interpreting what they encounter. Clearly such a belief immediately lends itself more readily to qualitative research approaches, and, because unlike the positivist epistemology it doesn't claim to be value neutral, it is regarded as much more subjective and opinion-based.

Critical

Critical epistemology (or critical social research epistemology) aims to challenge both the positivist and interpretivist epistemologies. It does not necessarily avoid science, or claims to be scientific, but does not claim to be a value-neutral process. Instead, critical social researchers would assert that all research is underpinned by values. It will also not necessarily avoid interpretation, instead it intends to locate itself within a more balanced position. Critical social research believes that research should be to reveal the processes through which dominant understandings of the world are constructed. As an approach it promotes the use of a variety of research methods, believing that what is most important is that the methods selected are the most appropriate to the issue that is being studied. Critical social research attempts to shed light upon the way in which the dominant ideas and understanding of the world are created and maintained. It regards all knowledge as socially produced. The critical epistemology attempts to 'see the bigger picture'.

Epistemologies

	Positivism	Interpretivism	Critical
Assumptions about the nature of the social world that is under study	• There is an objective external reality that can be discovered by research	• There is no 'objective reality' because we construct reality in a social context. What counts as 'real' are those things that we are conscious of	• Accepts that reality is constructed, but in different ways, and at different times, and different places. However this does not mean that these constructions do not have real effects upon people. Some constructions become dominant and inform the way our society is structured
Epistemological assumptions – that is, assumptions about how we should generate knowledge	• Knowledge of the social world should be gained in the same way that scientists gain knowledge of the natural world. It should be based upon the collection of 'fact' and through the testing of hypothesis	• The social world is completely different to the natural world; and we cannot treat people as objects. Therefore knowledge must be gained via interpretation – what meaning do people attach to their experiences?	• We have to understand the ways and processes in which we come to understand the world. We need to consider how society is structured and in whose interest. Research needs to make inequalities visible and challenge 'common sense'

(Continued)

(Continued)

	Positivism	Interpretivism	Critical
	• Key concepts: explanation, objectivity	• Key concepts: Interpretation, meaning, subjectivity	• Key concepts: theoretical understanding; objectivity (but that doesn't mean value freedom – we all have values)
Preference in terms of research methodology	• Quantitative methods and hypothesis testing	• Qualitative methods	• Methods are selected according to the question

All too often in criminological research there is a tendency to simply promote one method (quantitative or qualitative) and criticise the other. Too often it could be believed that there exist only two epistemological traditions (positivism and interpretivism) with academics attaching themselves to one tradition and attacking the other.

Ethics

Ethical concerns in research are about the principals that inform our research practices. Social scientists use the term 'ethics' to describe and debate what we deem appropriate and inappropriate during the research process. Such concerns have always played a major part of all forms of social research. It is difficult to talk generally about ethics, because what is ethical and what is not will depend to some extent upon individual values, attitudes and beliefs (that stated, while we will all have different opinions on matters involving ethics, we have an obligation to consider the ethical implications of our work).

There is a general consensus amongst criminologists, for example, regarding anonymity to be afforded to informants, consent to be sought wherever possible. This openness (sometimes described as overt research) may still vary because even if one is overt and open about the research, how much detail they give will vary. As criminological research often involves some degree of risk, or the researcher would not be granted permission or consent of those people or organisations they wish to study, or a combination of both of these considerations, some criminologists chose the opposite approach (that is, covert research). Covert research is secretive, and participants will not be aware that they are being observed, and in some cases the researcher may even going so far as to deliberately deceive or lie in order to keep the research secretive. Clearly the methodology will be somewhat dependant upon the 'ethical' principles to which individual or groups of researchers subscribe, and the validity of each method is an ethical judgement that only the researcher can make.

> *When we consider research (whether conducting it or commenting upon it) it is important that we consider not only what the research tells us, but the ethics that informed the study and potential ethical dilemmas that the findings of the research might raise.*

Access

Access is a term that we use in criminology to describe gaining permission or admittance to conduct study. This might sound simple but we should not forget that in almost all research, access will be a recurring theme, for example, each time you meet potential informants you will have to re-negotiate access. Gaining access can involve gaining access to an individual (e.g. a prison governor) or a group (e.g. prison officers) or to an agency (e.g. the prison service more generally). Access may also involve documents (e.g. pre-sentence reports). In criminological research access can be one of the most important considerations – we must ask questions about access, who gains access to conduct research, and more importantly, how and why?

The politics of criminological research

It is important to remember that research does not take place in a void, and that there will be a vast number of factors that will influence research processes. Just as the criminal justice system will be linked to a vast amount of political and ideological arguments, so will research. The challenge that 'critical' and 'interpretivist' epistemologies have made to the notion of value-freedom in social research has been very significant. There are few social scientists who continue to argue that when research is produced it should be wholly value-neutral, and most criminologists will now acknowledge (some happily, some more reluctantly) that their research is not value-free.

Criminologists must be aware that the research they undertake can potentially have an impact upon both criminal justice policy and practices, for better and for worse! In criminological research there are essentially a number of areas where political considerations may be of influence and the following should be remembered.

In researching crime and deviance, criminologists are dealing with subject matter that is commonly regarded as socially problematic, and therefore it is something that is likely to be subject to political discussion, policy and initiatives. Criminological researchers are also involved in numerous political processes on a smaller scale because research often seeks to understand the standpoints of differing, sometimes oppositional groups, regardless of whether one subscribes to the concept of value neutrality or not.

❝What are the strengths of quantitative and qualitative research? Can you think of a research project that would be best suited to i) qualitative methods ii) quantitative methods iii) both quantitative and qualitative methods?❞

When addressing this type of question you should clearly demonstrate a knowledge of the differences between each research approach, and be able to identify where each is suitable. You should also remember that increasingly, criminologists are combining methods to generate the most accurate research possible. Remember that using examples from recent research projects will almost always be beneficial. Remember that qualitative and quantitative methods lend themselves to different tasks, and you can illustrate this with examples.

Taking it **FURTHER**

Examples of current research (both quantitative and qualitative) can be accessed through the Home Office Research Development and Statistics Department website (see www.homeoffice.gov.uk/rds/index.htm). Look at some examples and ask yourself whether the research supports the assertions that the criminologist in question is making. What might be the benefit/drawback of their methodology? Also think in some detail about what the researcher has said: What might have lead them to their conclusions? Will they be based solely upon research evidence generated, upon the researchers personal beliefs and values, or might economic/political factors have played a part?

Textbook guide

There are numerous good books and chapters in books on the subject of criminological research. Students should see Leslie Noak and Emma Wincup's (2004) edited collection *Criminological research: understanding qualitative method* as an excellent introduction to qualitative research in criminology. Victor Jupp et al.'s edited collection *Doing Criminological Research* (2000) and Victor Jupp's *Methods of Criminological Research* (1989) are also informative texts. More generally Tim May's (2001) *Social Research* is now in its third edition and is a comprehensive overview of the issues involved in undertaking social research generally, and would provide an excellent source of additional reading for those new to the social sciences.

2.3

locating crime within the individual: biological and psychological approaches

Core areas: **Positivism in criminology**

Early criminology inspired by positivism

Early biological criminology

Psychological theories

Why are biological and psychological theories influential?

Running themes

Biological and psychological criminology has searched for causes of crime. The **research methods** that inform such studies and the **evidence** that they present must be examined carefully. Biological and psychological criminology can present persuasive arguments, but they can also contain very **discriminatory** ideas about issues such as **race, sex** and **gender** that could lead to **inequality**. We therefore also have to question what the **practical application** of these theories may be.

Common pitfall: A problem that arises in criminology when we create categories and terms is that they are not fixed or universally agreed upon (although some textbooks suggest they are). This can often cause confusing differences when two criminologists use different terms to describe what is actually the same theory.

Remember whilst psychological, sociological and biological theories are often separated in textbooks; the real world and real crime probably need to acknowledge elements of each. Psychological theories and biological theories need not ignore sociological factors.

It will help you if from the outset you do not worry too much about categories, but the core elements of theories. This involves asking, 'What is this theory concerned with? If we think just about categories we notice that psychological criminological theories tend to place emphasis upon factors such as emotional adjustment and personality, while sociological criminology is more likely to be concerned instead with, say, cultural values and status. Problems arise when these theories become mixed together, and this happens frequently.

Positivism in criminology

The decline of classicism can essentially be seen as mirroring the rise of a positivist criminology that claimed to promote the scientific study of society, and replace philosophical judgement and opinion with empirically grounded fact and science. Many criminological textbooks tell a conventional tale of an emerging new, scientific positivistic criminology banishing the philosophical thinking that preceded it, only to turn and ridicule this positivism in the next paragraph.

If you were to read many of the accounts of the emergence of biological positivism, this is what you might well expect to encounter. The reality however, is not so stark, and the distance that we have travelled from the frequently ridiculed biological positivism of Lombroso (and certainly psychological positivism) may not be so far as we would like to think. In reality it is difficult in many ways to see any real decline in the principal arguments of classical and early positivist criminology. Consider for one minute the opinions you have heard expressed on the subject of crime. I am certain that 'choice' or 'freewill' would be familiar concepts, as may a lack of choice. As a counter to this, positivism held that for some people there may be factors that propelled them toward crime. Positivism in criminology sought to explain and predict future patterns of social behaviour, using secondary statistical data, and later, methods linked with knowledge of medicine, psychiatry and psychology. It tends to be associated with the scientific commitment to finding facts on the cause of crime. Positivistic research forms the basic methodology for a vast array of criminological research that is undertaken in accordance with positivistic principles, such as deductive reasoning, striving for value-neutrality in research, generating and testing hypotheses through measurement, and ensuring research is objective.

Positivism is a research method and not a specific branch of criminology! Positivism spans biological, psychological and sociological attempts to identify key causes of crime. These are then often presented as 'causal factors' of crime, largely regarded as outside the individuals' control. Therefore positivism can tend to regard criminality as pre-determined rather than chosen. It is often seen as contrasting with many of the arguments made by the classical school of criminology. The table below contrasts the core principles of positivism and classicism.

Classicism	Positivism
Humans are rational beings and their actions can be understood as 'freewill'	Human actions are to a large extent, determined by forces beyond an individual's control
Crime can be regarded as an error of rational judgement or a mistake	Individuals are propelled towards crime by biological, sociological and psychological factors over which they have little control
Punishment can act as a deterrent	Treatment can assist in preventing further offending
The punishment should fit the offence	Treatment should be tailored to fit the specific needs of the offender

Early criminology inspired by positivism

Key thinker

Cesare Lombroso (1836–1909) was founder of the 'Italian Positivist School', Lombroso was a medical physician whose major work *L'Uomo Delinquente* (*The Criminal Man*) was first published in 1876. Lombroso put forward the idea (based on research on offenders) that there were different types of criminal, including the 'born criminal' who was a throwback to an earlier stage of evolution, and was therefore socially inferior to normal people. Lombroso termed this 'atavism' and suggested that there were atavistic stigma present on the bodies of criminals that could be identified and measured. He was heavily influenced by positivism in terms of his methodology, producing what is termed anthropometrical research (this describes attempts to derive character traits by measuring features of the body) that was quantitative in nature.

Early biological criminology

Many criminological textbooks acknowledge Lombroso as founder of criminology, which is interesting given that at the time of Lombroso's writing he was only one of a group of professionals and interested parties who had turned their attentions to the study of the criminal (admittedly many did not claim to adopt the scientific rigour that Lombroso suggested of his work).

The growth of imprisonment as a punishment had supplied prison surgeons with subjects to observe. In *Criminal Sociology*, Ferri (one of Lombroso's students) mentions a number of works generated prior to Lombroso's publication of *The Criminal Man*. These observations were also not restricted to studies of the body. In *The Decent of Man*, Charles Darwin noted the influence of psychologist Dr. Prosper Despine, who he suggested as early as 1868, gave 'many curious cases of the worst criminals, who apparently have been entirely destitute of conscience' (1871: 78). Many of the very first explanations of criminal and deviant behaviour were biological, and certainly, much early criminological research was positivistic in its method and the preserve of the medically trained and educated classes.

Remember that positivism is a research method and not a distinct strand of criminological thought. Therefore you should perhaps try, where possible, to avoid talking about 'positivist criminology' in a general sense. Can the work of Lombroso really be compared to, say, a study of street lighting on a council estate in the 1980s that uses a positivistic methodology?

While Lombroso's work could be placed under the heading of biological criminology, investigations of the causes of criminality using more sophisticated research methods examining biological criminological theories have continued to be developed in the twentieth century. These have examined:

- Intelligence (which suggest that offenders have mostly low IQ)
- Genetic abnormalities
- Hyper-masculinity and the aggressive male
- The influence of testosterone (a hormone that can increase aggression)
- Adrenaline (another hormone)
- Neurotransmitters (substances like serotonin and dopamine that transmit signals between neurons and the brain)
- Heredity and potential transfer of criminal tendencies (by studying twins and those who have been adopted)
- Factors related to nutrition (such as blood sugar levels, vitamins and minerals) and any potential influence on levels of criminality.

All have a biological component and all are based upon 'scientific' research. Much as Lombroso searched for physical cause of crime, these studies have shared that concern. Yet whilst biological explanations may explain why some individuals do commit crime, they can never explain all criminal behaviour (although some confidently suggest they have, for example, criminologist Johannes Lange (1931) was convinced criminality was inherited from parents – he titled his book *Crime as Destiny*).

The weaknesses of biological explanations can be offset somewhat if criminologists and researchers look at the interplay of biological, psychological and social approaches (as a few have), creating a more unified approach to the study of crime. That stated, biological explanations of crime still display a tendency to make grand claims based on little evidence. Biological theories have also fuelled cultural myths such as the perceptions of racially inferior groups and irrational women (women have often been regarded as more prone to biologically influenced behaviour than men). They have also led to the development of eugenics, which proposes removal or containment of those deemed to be inferior (for example, in Nazi Germany which targeted non-white races, homosexuals, gypsies, Jews, the mentally ill and the physically disabled).

> I have suggested that criminological theory was influenced by ideological considerations. What should we do if we found that it was possible to predict as accurately as 97% of murderers by finding a 'murder gene'? The answer you would give cannot be fact, but is based upon personal values and beliefs.

Biological criminology has proved very influential, and has not always been associated with the most extreme forms of treatment. It could be argued, that the positivistic drive has increased the influence of experts keen to 'treat' and 'rehabilitate' offenders. We refer to this as 'the treatment paradigm' (essentially the idea that criminals should be treated rather than punished).

Psychological theories

Key thinker

Hans Eysenck (1916–97) is best known (in terms of his criminological work) for *Crime and Personality* (1964). Eysenck was a British psychologist (although he was actually born in Berlin during the First World War) who suggested that personality is biologically determined. Having trained under Cyril Burt, Eysenck believed that it was possible to chart the human personality on scales of three core components: extroversion, neuroticism and psychoticism. He believed that exaggeration of these personality traits could lead to greater propensity toward anti-social behaviour.

Psychological criminology

Another aspect of criminology that locates the cause of crime primarily within the individual is psychology (although some psychology falls into the category of social psychology which acknowledges concepts such as identity, thinking and small group influences that may be external to the individual). Psychology is a term usually used to mean the study of someone's mind or spirit (although sometimes animals are also studied under these heading). More specifically psychology is associated with an individual's personality, reasoning, thought, intelligence, learning, perception, imagination, memory and creativity. As with biological theories it is important to remember that psychological theories often make reference to factors that exist outside of the individual. That stated, the core causation of criminality is regarded as existing principally within the individual's 'personality'.

Within the general psychological theories of crime (although it is a theory that is not exclusively concerned with psychology), a most noted thinker was Hans Eysenck. In his work *Crime and Personality* (1964), which is regarded as a work of psychology, Eysenck developed a theory of crime and the causation of crime that linked biological and sociological influences with the development of an individual's personality. Eysenk believed that some people would be more inclined towards anti-social behaviour because of their personality.

Hans Eysenck's *Crime and Personality* (1964)

- Eysenck's theory incorporates biological, social and individual factors
- He thought that through genetic transmission, some individuals are born with abnormalities of the brain and nervous system that will affect their ability to learn from, or condition themselves to, the environment around them
- Most children learn to control their behaviour by developing a 'conscience'
- People have three dimensions of personality: Extroversion (E), Neuroticism (N) and Psychoticism (P)
- These dimensions are all charted on a scale (think of a line) that runs between low and high. Most people will fall in the middle range – there will be relatively few people at the extreme ends of the scales
- Extroverts are under aroused, and therefore someone who is high E will be impulsive and seek stimulation
- Neuroticism concerns emotions. People who are low N are stable, calm and even tempered (even under stress) while in contrast someone who is a high N would be moody and anxious
- Psychoticism is difficult to define, but it assesses attributes such as a liking for solitude, aggression and tough mindedness that again range from low to high
- The speed of people's ability to develop conscience is influenced by their ability to be conditioned, which will depend upon their personality
- High E and high N individuals are most difficult to condition
- Low N and Low E are the most receptive to conditioning
- Those with strong anti-social tendencies will score high on all three scales.

Eysnecks work blended psychological theories with other influences, something that is shared by a great deal of more recent psychological criminology. Indeed it is worth stressing the point that psychology could be linked to any number of other criminological theories. Theories that stress the influence of societal factors, such as economic pressures, peer group influences and self-perception, all rely to some extent upon the way an individual perceives themselves (and therefore must acknowledge the individual's psychology).

More contemporary studies that have attempted to link criminality to individual psychology have attempted to make clear links with other factors, be that sociological, environmental, biological, or a combination of all three. Right-wing American criminologist James Q. Wilson (who is a prominent right realist) produced a general psychological theory of crime in collaboration with Richard J. Herrnstein (a Harvard University professor in psychology). They turned their attention to early social circumstances and family influences in *Crime and Human Nature* (1984).

Wilson and Herrnstein view that crime is a rational act of a defective personality. They argue that crime occurs when the rewards (be they material gains, peer approval, emotional gratification, or a sense of justice restored) exceed the costs of imprisonment, pangs of conscience, shame, and so forth. They assert that people differ in how they calculate risks and benefits; to unravel that crucial difference, they analyse a range of factors: sociological, psychological and environmental.

Ultimately Wilson and Herrnstein reject biological notion of the existence of a specific gene for criminality. Rather, they postulate that a particular personality type, with features that make a person more likely to value crime, is more likely to be responsible. These features, which the authors call 'constitutional factors', are either inborn or emerge very early in life and are only minimally influenced by family, even less by culture and economy. For instance, Wilson and Herrnstein regard impulsiveness and the inability to contemplate the long-term consequences of one's actions as a critical element of the criminal personality. Criminals are stunted in their ability to weight either the costs to be exacted or the future benefits and consequently they opt for the immediate emotional and material gratification.

Psychology has become massively influential in criminology, a fact to which an array of recent textbooks attests. The fact that some training and basic knowledge of psychology has become almost a pre-requisite for those working in the statutory agencies of the criminal justice system may be seen to prove its practical usefulness. Psychology still has much to offer criminologists, as Peter Ainsworth has suggested, 'of all the academic disciplines that have examined crime and its causation, psychology seems best placed to help investigators to understand the behaviour of those individuals who commit serious crime' (2001: 184).

Why are biological and psychological theories influential?

- Biological positivism, and most psychological criminology, locate the cause of crime *predominantly* within the individual (and not therefore in economic or social conditions). It is therefore politically useful as it deflects attention away from the demand to improve social and economic conditions

- Psychiatry as a discipline advanced and gained prestige, providing a suitable backdrop for notions of 'treatment'
- The concepts are connected with prejudices and fears about 'dangerous classes' amongst more respectable classes, especially in expanding cities in the early twentieth century
- It offers new possibilities for scientific, humane and expert control and regulation of the population for those in power (governments), when other options seemingly are not working
- The move towards incarceration as the principal method for dealing with offenders means that there are both subjects for study available (prisoners), and a purpose in studying them to try and inform knowledge and practice
- Almost all criminological theories can be linked with psychology in some way, whilst biological features are hidden and cannot easily be proved or disproved for the majority of offenders.

⁴⁴ Consider the strength of the argument that criminals are 'born not made'. ⁷⁷

This type of question would immediately allow you to show knowledge of the development of criminology, and you should remember that you can make reference to Lombroso and his work. However you should also consider the whole range of factors that can influence criminality (using the upcoming chapters). Remember there is very little to suggest that criminals may be born, but there have been a range of recent criminology that investigates biological factors and you might want to read further and develop some knowledge of relevant contemporary studies (try using the list of biological criminology as a guide).

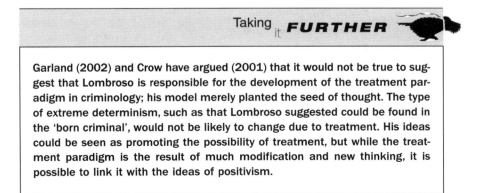

Taking it *FURTHER*

Garland (2002) and Crow have argued (2001) that it would not be true to suggest that Lombroso is responsible for the development of the treatment paradigm in criminology; his model merely planted the seed of thought. The type of extreme determinism, such as that Lombroso suggested could be found in the 'born criminal', would not be likely to change due to treatment. His ideas could be seen as promoting the possibility of treatment, but while the treatment paradigm is the result of much modification and new thinking, it is possible to link it with the ideas of positivism.

Textbook guide

Exerts from Lombroso and Eysenck's works are available in McLaughlin et al.'s *Criminological Perspectives* (2003). David Garland's *Of Crimes and Criminals: The Development of Criminology in Britain* in McGuire et al. (2002) is a good historical account of the development of criminology. More generally a number of textbooks give comprehensive coverage of the subjects of biological and psychological criminology. For psychology, Ron Blackburn's (1993) *The Psychology of Criminal Conduct* is complex, but an extremely valuable contribution. Students who would like to seek to understand more of the influence of psychological approaches and the current thoughts on offender treatment, will be unlikely to find a better account that Iain Crow's *The Treatment and Rehabilitation of Offenders* (2001).

2.4

crime as external to the individual: sociological theories

Core areas: **Consensus theories**

Conflict theories

Feminist perspectives

Social disorganisation

Differential association

Strain

Status frustration

Differential opportunity

Neutralisation

Drift

Control theory

Labelling/interactionist/new deviancy theories

Running themes

As most of the theories described below stem from the work of sociologists, they have tended to show a greater awareness of **inequality**, **power**, **class**, **sex and gender**, **race**, **ideology**, **representation**, **discrimination** and **justice** than concern with finding 'causes of crime'. They have also very often (though not always) relied upon different **research methods** to biological and psychological criminology, instead promoting qualitative research with those who offend.

Key thinkers

There are quite simply too many influential studies to isolate and examine only a couple of contributions, and therefore I have listed what I consider to be some seminal works. I would draw your attention to the following theorists (although this list is far from exhaustive)

- Becker (1963)
- Cloward and Ohlin (1960)
- Cohen (1955)
- Durkheim (1895)
- Gottfredson and Hirschi (1990)
- Hirschi (1969)
- Lemert (1972)
- Matza (1964)
- Merton (1938 and 1968)
- Quinney (1970 and 1974)
- Shaw and McKay (1942)
- Sutherland (1931)
- Sutherland and Cressey (1978)
- Sykes and Matza (1957)
- Taylor, Walton and Young (1973)
- Tennenbaum (1938)

The previous section explored attempts by criminologists of both the psychological and biological school, to locate the causes of crime specifically within the individual. Such a focus often suggests that there are identifiable differences between offenders and non-offenders. This chapter is devoted to those criminological theorists who have proposed that criminality can perhaps best be understood with reference to social circumstances and factors external to the individual.

Consensus theories

Example: Durkheim (1895)

Several versions of these theories thrived in both Europe and America between the late nineteenth century until the 1950s. These theories sought to explain laws against crime as expressions of a consensus of social and moral views. The functionalist view suggests that although crime and deviance are problematic, they can also play an important role in pushing forward moral boundaries. Therefore functionalists can regard crime as a price worth paying for the possibility of progress (this idea is most prominently associated with Emile Durkheim). Consensus and functionalist views take for granted that criminals exist who must be controlled, and do not seek to explain why people behave in the way that they do (although criminal behaviour is not regarded as pathological or abnormal).

Conflict theories

Examples: Sellin (1938); Vold (1958); Quinney (1970; 1977); and Taylor, Walton and Young (1973)

There have been several versions of conflict theory, which can be regarded as originating in the 1950s, but gained increasing prominence in the 1960s. Like consensus and functionalist approaches, conflict theories are interested in the role that the law serves, and why some things are defined as crime whilst others are not. A number of conflict theorists are mentioned previously, as they contributed a great deal to debates about what crime is (see Chapter 2.4 for examples of conflict theorists). Conflict theories can be divided into groups. Conflict theory in the 1960s became heavily linked with Marxist theory, and tended to emphasise a single dominant source of power that is rooted in control of wealth, but able to influence the ideology of crime and control through the mass media. From the 1960s onward, Marxist criminology and Neo-Marxist theory informed the development of **left idealist** or **radical** criminology. This was an approach informed by sociological theory that sought to take crime seriously, but still analyse why some people and some actions were deemed criminal, and the role of the state and the powerful in this process. Left idealists believed that research should be critical, and seek to highlight the divisions in society. That stated, Marxism has become an unfashionable theoretical basis, and few criminologists would now suggest that they were left idealist in their theoretical perspective. In the 1990s, conflict theories focused more upon issues of racial discrimination and institutional racism in the processing of Black and Asian offenders. In Britain the best example is still Taylor, Walton and Young's *The New Criminology* (1973) and in America, Richard Quinney's 1970 and 1974 studies.

Feminist perspectives

Examples: Adler (1975) and Smart (1976)

There is not a single feminist theory of crime. Feminism draws from other theories (especially conflict theory) to describe the way females are affected by the criminal justice system (both women's experiences as offenders and victims). The reason that we refer to feminist perspectives (and not feminist theory) is that there are many different versions of feminism. Feminists also often make use of the concept of 'patriarchy', to describe the structural oppression of women that exists within society.

Although there are a range of feminist perspectives, almost all feminist perspectives share a concern with the inequality of women, discrimination against them and an insistence that, all too often, theories neglect women, and assume that theories about male behaviour are applicable to the experiences of women.

From the 1970s feminist criminologists argued that criminology either neglected women, or explained women's behaviour in stereotypical and discriminatory ways. For example, they highlighted the fact that biological explanations were still being applied to women that had long been discredited as explanations for male criminal behaviour. Feminists also raised questions about whether women were unfairly treated by the criminal justice system, for example, by getting longer sentences for less serious offences. That stated, the extent to which the criminal justice system discriminates against women is contested, and feminist theorists are still very influential in criminology.

Similarly gender debates have not been restricted to why women commit crime, but have also questioned why men disproportionately commit more crime, and whether this may be because of crime's potential for re-enforcing a masculine image. Many of these are not written by female feminists but by males who endorse feminist philosophy and take a pro-feminist stance (both these aspects are examined in more detail in Chapter 2.9).

Social disorganisation

Example: Shaw and McKay (1942)

Those who subscribe to social disorganisation theory suggest that stability and integration into society produce conformity in people. Conversely, disorder and poor integration can permit and encourage crime.

The Chicago School of Sociology

Social disorganisation theory is linked with the University of Chicago's School of Sociology (often referred to as the Chicago School) and originated in the 1920s. A number of influential sociologists/criminologists from the Chicago School used social disorganisation theory in their work (there are a number of examples in other chapters: Shaw and McKay (1942), Thrasher, (1927), Sutherland (1939), to name but some). The influence of the Chicago School could be seen as two-fold: The University of Chicago contribution to criminology often begins by acknowledging the work of Robert E. Park and Earnest W. Burgess. Park was an influential figure who encouraged students to undertake qualitative research in the field. Burgess is perhaps more notable as a criminologist than Park, having taught the first criminology and delinquency courses at the University of Chicago. Park and Burgess (with McKenzie) authored *The City* in 1925 – this book introduced the theory of 'concentric circles' upon which the theory of social disorganisation is built.

I have known a number of criminology courses set assignments where students are asked to evaluate the contribution of the Chicago School to criminology. The role of the Chicago school was not simply social disorganisation and a lasting focus upon the link between the environment and crime. Chicago theorists were instrumental in promoting qualitative research methods e.g. Thrasher and participant observation (1927): Shaw and life history (1930). The Chicago School's contribution to criminology in terms of research methods should not be overlooked!

Social disorganisation is most readily associated with ecological studies of delinquency undertaken by Clifford R. Shaw and Henry D. McKay (1942), which in turn owes much to the rapid expansion of Chicago as a city, and links patterns of juvenile delinquency to patterns of urban development and the expansion of the city. Delinquency and deviance were regarded as higher in areas near the city centre. At the heart of the city was industry and business, but as the city grew, these businesses encroached into what were once residential areas. The area that surrounds the city, the 'zone of transition', was often associated with migrant groups that were the most recent arrivals to the city. This area was characterised by the poorest (often rented) housing, physical decay, broken communities, a shifting and transient population and high rates of illegitimate birth. Those from the Chicago School suggested that crime was not the result of biological and psychological abnormalities. Instead, Chicago theorists believed that crime and deviance were normal responses to these abnormal environmental circumstances. They suggested that crime could be 'culturally transmitted' across generations, and that industrialisation, urbanisation and to some extent migration (and the resulting lack of attachment to community and institutions) undermine stability.

The policy implications of accepting social disorganisation essentially involve working in communities, particularly high delinquency areas, increasing informal social control, encouraging young people to form an attachment to their community, and challenging delinquent energies into legitimate leisure pursuits. Whilst social disorganisation is not empirically proven, much would seem to support what people think. Researchers are still influenced by the link between urban development and environment and crime, with modern crime prevention researchers paying a great deal of attention to environment and crime.

Differential association

Examples: Sutherland (1939); Sutherland and Cressey (1978)

Chicago School sociologist, Edwin Sutherland made many contributions to criminology, one of which is the concept of differential association. It was Sutherland alone (1939) and in collaboration with Cressey (1978) who suggested that criminal behaviour was learnt and transmitted. He was influenced by a desire that criminology examine crime as socially harmful, and include the crime of the socially elite (see Chapter 2.11).

Differential association theory asserts that criminal behaviour is learned rather than inherited or invented by individuals. It is learned in social interaction, often within intimate social groups. Differential association suggests that a person becomes delinquent because of an excess of definition as favourable to violations of law (as opposed to unfavourable) from their surrounding subculture. Differential association also suggests that the process of learning by association with criminal and anti-criminal patterns does not involve imitation alone. The longer or more frequently an individual is exposed to attitudes and behaviour, the more affect that attitude or behaviour is likely to have upon the individual. Sutherland did not suggest that the goals or desires of offenders were different to those of society more generally, simply that they had different ways of achieving their aims.

> *Differential association stresses the interactions between individuals and the influence of significant others upon them, but also stresses the importance of learning. It has, therefore, a physiological component and is often regarded as psychological criminology. It is consequently one example of the difficulty in separating theories into categories under broad headings.*

Strain

Example: Merton (1938; 1968)

Anomie is a concept that stems from the work of functionalist Emile Durkheim, and means a state of confusion about social rules and values that is often caused by rapid social change. Durkheim first developed the concept as part of his attempt to explain suicide, but in terms of criminology it is perhaps more relevant to turn to the work of sociologist Robert Merton, who in America set out to explain the reasons for crime being concentrated in lower-class areas, and in lower-class and minority groups. He also sought to explain why America had such a high crime rate.

Merton argued that there was an inequality between culturally-approved goals in society (an example of a goal is that all men are encouraged to persue success in terms of wealth and status) and the means of achieving those goals (the means of achieving wealth and status, through say education and employment, are not open to everyone). Merton argued that this disparity (or strain) between means and goals drove some of those denied the legal or legitimate means, to turn to illegal means. Therefore strain creates frustration and resentment, and this is the motive for crime.

Robert Agnew is one of the theorists inspired by Merton's concept of strain, and he attempted to focus more directly upon the impact of 'strain' upon individuals (1992). Agnew reworked Merton's notion of strain into three types, and produced a version of strain theory that paid more attention to the psychological impacts of strain.

In terms of policy, the existence of strain can lead to a promotion of social justice, trying to provide for an equality of opportunity for all, and promotion of less competitiveness.

Status frustration

Examples: Cohen (1955); Agnew (1992); Messerschmidt (1993)

Linking with strain and the concept of anomie is the notion of status frustration. This concept is in essence descended from strain and deals with the way illegitimate rather than legitimate activities are endorsed by some groups (which often includes the lower class, the disadvantaged and excluded minorities who feel the wrongness of being denied the legitimate opportunities that others have). Status frustration is informed by a need to aspire to a form of behaviour that weakens any commitment to lead a law-abiding life.

Evidence which supports this notion is often qualitative and ethnographic, conforming to what is referred to as gang and subculture studies. For example, Albert Cohen (1955) was particularly interested in the crimes of delinquent males who often offended together. Particularly, Cohen provides some explanation as to why there exists a 'delinquent subculture' amongst lower-class males. His work was conducted in America in the 1950s. Cohen suggested that lower-class males in that society often could not aspire, legally, to the material standards of the middle class in terms of dress, behaviour, educational success and gainful employment. Cohen argued that this denied them status in society and could serve to lower their self-esteem. He argued that in particular, lower-class males came into contact with middle-class values in school. Here they had a choice. They could conform (and possibly become losers), or they could reject the standards of the middle class, and celebrate and enact the opposite values. Cohen argued that young lower-class males could invert the values of middle-class society and thereby created their own system of standards, which created self-esteem. The motives for delinquent behaviour are anger and resentment. In creating their own subculture, young lower-class males place value upon meeting the expectation of peers rather than teachers and parents. Subcultures become self-reinforcing, a permanent alternative to middle-classes standards. Therefore 'status frustration' contributes to delinquency, with youngsters offending out of 'malice' and 'for the hell of it'. Status frustration can also cross with subjects such as masculinity and crime, and James Messerscmidt's concepts of young men offending to 'do masculinity' (1993) also fits this model.

Differential opportunity

Example: Cloward and Ohlin (1960)

In the 1960s in America, Richard Cloward and Lloyd Ohlin contributed their perspective to the debate about lower-class youth subcultures with the theory of 'differential opportunity'. Their theory attempted to bridge the Merton **strain theory** and Sutherland **differential association** (interestingly, Ohlin had formerly studied under Sutherland, whilst Cloward had been taught by Merton).

Cloward and Ohlin believed that Cohen may have been right about subcultures possessing different values to those of the middle class, but there was more than one type of subculture. Similarly, while influenced by Merton, Cloward and Ohlin questioned whether everyone denied opportunity to legitimate success could in fact turn to illegitimate means. They believed that there were variations in the availability of illegitimate means to people. While Sutherland had argued that criminality was caused by differential association. They suggested that delinquent subcultures were based upon different opportunities that existed in different neighbourhoods. They suggested three separate subcultures (two of which were for society's excluded losers), see below.

Differential opportunity suggests three separate subcultures

Criminal	Conflict	Retreatist
(Making a living)	(Gang fighting)	(Drugs and alcohol)

All of the theories derived from 'anomie' tend to predict higher rates of delinquency in lower-class and excluded groups. Whilst official statistics would seem to support this assertion, official statistics are notoriously unreliable (see Chapter 2.6). There are a number of reasons why crime might be seen as more common in lower-class males – most notably that it is young lower-class males that live in the areas that the police tend to go looking for crime. It is also true that those from lower-class and disadvantaged backgrounds tend to be treated more harshly than their middle-class counterparts (e.g. they are more likely to be prosecuted, and more likely to receive more serious sanctions).

Self-report studies (mass surveys that are undertaken in confidence) show some minor youthful offending is distributed quite evenly across social class (although serious and persistent crime that tends to continue into adulthood is more common amongst the disadvantaged). There are problems with self-report studies, but the contradiction that this presents is an interesting one. There are also problems with the terms that are used. Disadvantaged and excluded are often linked to unemployment, however there is little evidence that suggests that unemployment alone leads to crime.

Anomie might also tend to exaggerate the extent to which people are passive actors influenced by society's goals. Many ordinary people may not take seriously the glamorous goals of society and instead measure themselves against more realistic and achievable goals – therefore not feeling aggrieved or frustrated. In terms of class and the definitions of class, perhaps the definitions of 'middle' and 'working class' are too general, how we define class is debatable, and there may be overlaps between class groups and values. Similarly, anomie theories tend to be predominantly urban in terms of their scope, and do not really tend to sit comfortably with urbanised, westernised society. In terms of scope it is questionable as to whether anomie theories seek to explain general patterns of criminal activity or the 'criminal careers' of individuals. Similarly, the criminologists that produced anomie linked to delinquent subcultures studied only men and boys, no one explained the differential distribution of crime between men and women – gender and its role in crime was not sufficiently explored. All of these factors serve to make the theories uncertain, even if to a large extent they may seem plausible and persuasive.

Neutralisation

Example: Sykes and Matza (1957)

Gresham Sykes and David Matza introduced their theory of neutralisation at the time when studies of subculture were most dominant, and theories based upon anomie were prevalent. Cohen and Cloward and Ohlin suggested that delinquents and criminals were able to act in such a way because they rejected society's 'norms' and 'values' and replaced them with their own value system. By obeying their own 'codes', which were different to those of mainstream society, criminals could feel no guilt. Sykes and Matza did not believe that this was the case. They did not believe that delinquents wholly rejected society's values, replacing them with their own; rather they simply found a way to get around them. The way they did this was by employing a series of attitudes that served to rationalise and justify their behaviour. These were 'techniques of neutralisation'.

Drift

Example: Matza (1964)

Matza built upon the 'techniques of neutralisation' with a more general theory that attempted to explain juvenile involvement in crime. He maintained the stance that total rejection of society's norms was not necessary for a delinquent to commit a criminal act. Highlighting the concept of freewill, Matza suggested that people could chose criminal and non-criminal actions. Matza argued that adolescents drift between conventional and criminal behaviour, not necessarily occupying one position, but instead choosing when to be criminal and when not to be. The techniques of neutralisation simply freed the individual from conventional society values and helped them to commit crime.

Control theory

Examples: Hirschi (1969); Gottfredson and Hirschi (1990)

Control theory approaches the issue of crime from a slightly different angle than many other criminological theories. It does not ask why people become criminals, but asks why people obey the law. The answer is to be found in control. People conform because they are controlled, and offend when this control breaks down. Control theory therefore tends to take crime for granted, as a given – people do not need a special motivation to commit a crime. Rather much like classicism, control theory suggests that anyone can offend, but sees individuals as even more self-interested and self-absorbed – 'anyone will violate the law if they think that they can get away with it'.

Control theory is most often associated with Travis Hirschi's *Causes of Delinquency* (1969) which used data gathered from a study of adolescent delinquents in California, and proposes 'delinquent acts result when an individual's bond to society is weak or broken' (1969: 16). Control theory can be used to explain any type of criminal behaviour or delinquency. It has been utilised and has influenced all manner of criminological discussion, and perhaps occupies the position of the most frequently discussed and tested of all criminological theories.

The core concept of control theory is the individual's bond to society. The bond has four component parts:

1 **Attachment** – including admiring and identifying with others so that we care about the expectations they have. The more insensitive an individual is to other people's expectations, the more they disregard their norms and the more likely they are to violate them. The concept of attachment is often linked to parenting

2 **Commitment** – the extent to which individuals have invested in conventional norms and have a stake in conformity, which might be jeopardised by crime. Essentially, the more someone has to lose, the less likely they are to risk criminality

3 **Involvement** – relating to the idea that the more preoccupied an individual is with accepted and conventional activities, the less likely they are to have the time, energy and contacts to get involved in unconventional activities. It follows that working, spending time with the family and participation in structured leisure activities all serve to reduce the likelihood to engage in criminality

4 **Agreement** – if a person finds the laws agreeable, they are less likely to break them. If a person endorses society's rules, they will not go against them (this component is termed conformity).

In his work, Hirschi supplied measurable criteria that could be used to evaluate individuals against all of the bonds. He tested his own theory and argued that the weaker the bonds, the higher the delinquency. Since the late 1960s, research has generally supported (to varying degrees) Hirschi's general propositions. That stated, whilst control theory might explain a significant proportion of delinquency, some people who are strongly attached offend, whilst those who are not, do not. Hirschi himself later rejected his own theory, and working jointly with Gottfredson (1990) moved toward a more simple theory of self-control arguing that people with low self-control commit more crime (low self-control involved poor socialisation especially poor child-rearing, poor quality of or lack of parental discipline, and was closely linked to the family).

Labelling/interactionist/new deviancy theories

Examples: Tennenbaum (1938); Becker (1963); Lemert (1972)

According to the interactionist school, crime and deviance can be explained as the result of a social reaction process that individuals go through in order to become deviant. It is rooted in symbolic interactionism, a sociological concept that suggests that individuals acquire their sense of 'self' through interacting with others.

Interactionist criminology is associated with Tennenbaum, Lemert and Becker. These theorists essentially argued that the labels given to deviants or offenders by those with power are a factor that can serve to re-enforce, and create criminality. Individuals can be dramatically stigmatised by the use of labels. The labels attached by the criminal justice system through court processes and sanctions, and the labels of the mental health system, are amongst the most powerful, and the label can serve to amplify deviance.

Perhaps the term labelling does not instantly appear in contemporary debates such as the stereotyping of black and female offenders, sex offenders and paedophiles, but it is possible to regard labelling as a precursor to these current concerns. Labelling is a very useful concept when any group are talked about in stereotypical terms.

All of the theories discussed above have a sociological component, that is, all recognise that crime is not simply a product of freewill, and that other factors that exist in society can impact upon an individual's propensity toward crime.

❝ How have sociological theories contributed to criminology? ❞

One of the problems that I tend to encounter with this type of question is that students will tend to try too hard and do too much in very little detail, rather than examine one or two theories in much greater detail. I would suggest that the latter approach is often better, as it allows you to convey an appreciation of one theory in detail. For example, you could take strain theory, talk about Merton, and then how Agnew built upon his work. You could make reference to the types of crime where strain may be evident. It is always far better, I feel, to be specific and show a good level of understanding of one theme.

Taking it *FURThER*

There are a wide range of sources mentioned in this chapter, which reflects the eclectic nature of criminology. I am firmly of the belief that students of criminology can benefit most from reading some of the original works mentioned above. That stated, I recognise that this is a time-consuming endeavour and therefore would recommend McLaughlin et al.'s *Criminological Perspectives* (2003) where you will encounter a number of extracts from works mentioned above.

Textbook guide

David Downes and Paul Rock's *Understanding Deviance* (1998) is a comprehensive textbook, and Katherine Williams also gives an excellent coverage in her *Textbook on Criminology* (2004). Those wishing to access a more interesting account of sociological contributions to criminology might consider Smith and Natalier's *Understanding Criminal Justice: Sociological Perspectives* (2004) as this contains some interesting contributions that are not acknowledged by many criminological textbooks.

2.5	
contemporary criminology	

Core areas: **Realism**

Right realism

Left realism

Administrative criminology

Peacemaking criminology

Cultural criminology

Journalism and offender accounts

Running themes

This chapter charts the development of some of the criminological theories that have emerged in recent years; and therefore I have termed it contemporary criminology. However, this should not be taken to signify that the theories in this chapter are any more or less relevant than those that you have encountered so far. Rather they are the more recent theories that have emerged in what is a constantly evolving academic subject. Due to the wide range of theories incorporated under this heading you should keep in mind the running themes generally and consider them in the context of each theory.

Key thinkers

This list is not meant as an exhaustive list of key thinkers (there are a great many names that could appear on this list!). Instead it seeks to direct you to some relevant contemporary examples:

- Wilson (1975)
- Murray (1990)
- Lea and Young (1984)
- Currie (1985)
- Clarke (1997)
- Felson and Clarke (1998)
- Cornish and Clarke (1996)
- Pepinsky and Quinney (1991)
- Katz (1988)
- Ferrell and Saunders (1995)
- Morrison (1998)
- Campbell (1993)
- James (2003)

Realism

Realist criminology tends to be either politically right or left in its ideology, but regardless of political affiliation, realist criminology shared some common beliefs about crime and its 'reality'. Essentially, as crime rates rose in Britain and North America from the 1960s onwards there was a concern that conflict theories and sociological explanations failed to address the causes.

Remember that realist criminology, whatever its political affiliation, shares in common a belief that:

- *Crime had risen from the 1960s in both America and Britain*
- *Crime is a problem which has a destructive and negative impact upon communities*
- *There is the need for academic criminologists to produce research that helps to develop realistic policy that will feed into practices that counter the 'crime problem'.*

Taking it **FURTHER**

It is difficult to understand the emergence of realism if you do not under-stand the way that law and order entered into political debate in Britain and America, but there are few texts that chart the politicisation of law and order. One exception is David Downes and Rod Morgan's chapter 'Dumping the "hostages to fortune"?' This appears in the second edition of the *Oxford Handbook of Criminology* (Maguire et al., 1997). It is well worth trying to access this through your university library as it provides an excellent overview of the politicisation of law and order.

Right realism

Examples: Wilson (1975); Wilson and Herrnstein (1984); Murray (1990)

Right realism (sometimes known as neo-conservative or neo-classical criminology) is associated principally with American academics such as James Q. Wilson and Charles Murray. Prominent right realists tend to have academic backgrounds in politics and political theory. This fostered a belief that there was a necessity for criminological theory to generate ideas that were useful to policy-makers.

Wilson believed that crime was a choice that followed the simple prin-ciples of economics – 'if crime pays more people will do it, if it pays less, less people will do it' (1975: 117). The way to achieve a reduction in crime therefore was to make crime pay less by the swift removal of society's per-sistent criminals for a significant proportion of their criminal career. Such action, argued Wilson, should lead to a changed perception amongst those likely to offend, and therefore crime would be less frequent.

Wilson's common-sense approach owed much to literary flair, and it has often been argued that his writing (and that of other right realists) is highly opinion based, with less emphasis placed upon evidence. Perhaps a counter to this is the fact that because many right realist thinkers come from 'philosophical' backgrounds there is less emphasis placed upon undertaking research, and so they are keen to generate arguments based upon moral reasoning and economics.

Another prominent right realist, Charles Murray, argued that in the lowest status groups in society, welfare dependency and 'fecklessness' had created a two tier system of poor. One group of poor were willing to advance themselves and adhere to society's values; the other type ('the underclass') were not. Murray located the causation of America and Britain's rising crime problem within this 'underclass'. The solution for Murray involved the retreat of state government, giving self-government opportunities to poor and affluent communities alike, and greater responsibility for the operation of institutions that affect their lives (1990). Whilst Murray's thesis on the underclass is doubtlessly impor-tant, he is also noted for advocating the effectiveness of imprisonment on the grounds of deterrence, and coined the phrase 'prison works' shortly before it was used by Michael Howard in his now famous speech at the Conservative Party Conference in 1993.

The key points of right realism

- *Crime is freely chosen (hence right realism is sometimes called right classicism)*
- *Minor crime leads to more substantial crimes, but hard line approaches that deter and prevent societal decline can also prevent crime*
- *Academic theory should be used to inform policy-making*
- *Crimes of the 'street' concern the public most and must be targeted*
- *The 'underclass' (welfare dependant, criminal and illegitimate) are those most responsible for rises in crime rates in Britain and America (Murray, 1990), however bothersome and unruly people (such as drunks, beggars and the mentally ill) also contribute (Wilson and Kelling, 1982)*
- *The state should withdraw from delivery of service and promote self-government with people having a greater say in services, but principles based upon deterrence are most effective in terms of criminal justice interventions*
- *Prison and 'zero tolerance' strategies are effective at reducing crime rates.*

Left realism

Examples: Lea and Young (1984); Currie (1985)

Left realism essentially stems from left idealist and conflict criminology, and began with criminologists in Britain, who in the 1980s proposed a shift toward a more 'realistic' stance on crime.

Left realists rejected what they saw as punitive and exclusionary policies that were endorsed by right realists and sought to counter to the growing influence of the mainly American right realists. They also rejected many of the policies of the right wing governments of Thatcher and Regan, but argued that 'conflict criminology' based upon Marxism, and labelling theories were unrealistic in their appraisal of crime (they believed such criminology displayed a tendency to shift attention from the actions of offenders, regarding them as victims). They promoted a politically left leaning view of crime, with a number of the left realists formerly having subscribed to left idealist principles (most notably Jock Young).

Like right realists, left realists agreed that crimes of the 'street' caused the public alarm and concern, and attempted to move away from some of the more radical political ideas associated with 'conflict' criminology.

Left realism differs from right realism in that it does not accept that choice and freewill are the sole factors in terms of causation of crime. They suggest that in order to study and understand crime, it needs to be broken down into four component parts (these form the square of crime, which is shown below). The square of crime represents the interconnected elements that constitute crime and therefore any analysis of crime must make reference to these components. Crime constitutes a social relationship between each four corners of the square. So, for example, the relationship between the state and the public determines the effectiveness of policing; the relationship between victim and offender will have an effect upon the impact of the crime; the relationship between offender and state will effect whether further crimes are committed; and the relationship between these four points will vary, dependant upon the crime.

The square of crime

State (Control-agencies)	Offender
Social Control	**Criminal Act**
The Public	**Victim/s**

A further key concept for the left realists was that of relative deprivation, which suggests that it is not the level or degree of poverty that caused crime, but it is the sense of injustice and disadvantage, which exclusion creates, that is instrumental in creating the conditions in which crime occurs. Left realism has been important in promoting the notion of 'social exclusion' which has been an ongoing concern of the government since 1997.

The key points of left realism

- Left realism attempts to find a middle ground between right realism and left idealism, criticising the exclusionary and punitive nature of the right, along with the unrealistic idealism of conflict and left idealist criminology
- Left realism had an evidence base which involved the use of victimisation surveys that suggested that the poorest and most excluded were those who most suffered the effects of crime. It regards 'relative deprivation' as a cause of crime, rather than poverty generally
- Left realism is an inclusive philosophy that acknowledges the contribution of subcultural theory, labelling theory, feminist and conflict theories
- Left realism suggests that the best responses to crime involve a variety of actors in social crime prevention, i.e. 'multi-agency' responses (although left realism also acknowledges that situational crime prevention and deterrent principles can be effective). Its long-term goal is to make long-term changes in the way society operates in terms of equality and justice, but similarly 'protect the public' on a day-to-day basis.

Administrative criminology

Examples: Clarke (1997); Felson and Clarke (1998); Cornish and Clarke (1996)

Administrative criminology gained influence in Britain from the late 1970s onward and is linked with realist approaches that sought practical solutions to the 'problem' of crime. Administrative criminology is so termed because of its links with governmental administration. Administrative criminology tends to have little interest in the causes of crime, endorsing the view of Wilson that crime is a rational and calculated choice made by offenders. The solution to crime for administrative criminologists such as Ron Clarke and Marcus Felson was to increase the chances of offenders being caught and to put in place measures that would be likely to increase the risks of being caught in the act of offending, or physically prevent offending (we term such approaches situational crime prevention).

Taking it ***FURTHER***

Marcus Felson is critical of those criminologists, who suggest that crime is socially constructed, arguing: 'Many criminologists believe that crime has no universal definition. They see crime as subjective, whereas society and its justice system "manufacture" crime by changing the definition. Their intellectual lawlessness makes a mess of our field' (Felson, 2002: 17). He is a fierce advocate of criminology having to offer practical solutions.

Like right and left realism, administrative criminology focuses exclusively upon street and property offences (street theft and robbery, car theft, assault and burglaries). It promotes community and individual responsibility for crime prevention, along with the perceived need to rethink the state's responses to crime, in order to make them more economically viable, more efficient and more effective. Administrative criminology is therefore aligned with research that attempts to ask 'what works?' in the context of offender treatment.

The key points of administrative criminology

- *Administrative criminology is a term that is used to describe criminology that refers to the act of committing the crime, and regards the criminal as a rational actor who will make choices*
- *It seeks not to solve a problem of crime, but find ways of preventing crime – or making crime a less attractive prospect for offender's through physical or psychological measures*
- *Administrative criminology is so termed due to its close ties with government, it tends to be positivistic in nature, and concerned with situational crime prevention and the efficiency and effectiveness of interventions.*

Peacemaking criminology

Example: Pepinsky and Quinney (1991)

The specific concept of 'peacemaking' in criminology was introduced in America by Harold Pepinsky and Richard Quinney in their book *Criminology as Peacemaking* (1991) but has had little, if any impact upon British criminology. They suggested that peacemaking criminology is drawn from three peacemaking traditions: religious, humanistic and feminist/critical.

The core concept of peacemaking criminology is the rejection of what is perceived to be an inherently violent and hierarchical criminal justice system that seeks to redress harm through harm and repress criminality through force. Peacemaking criminologists propose that an alternative, non-oppressive, and inclusive system would be more socially just and acceptable. I would assert that rather than thinking of peacemaking criminology as a new discipline, it is regarded as a long established tradition.

Peacemaking criminologists often reject the language and imagery that accompanies practices in criminal justice, such as the idea of a 'War on Drugs' or 'War on Crime' (which is often linked to right realist criminology) in favour of more considered 'ways of thinking, speaking, and writing that foster peace', their aim is to be 'a compassionate criminology' (Quinney, 1993: 4). Its ideology could also be regarded as being very much in line with restorative justice philosophies, and a number of current interventions could be regarded as conforming to the general ideas of peacemaking criminology (for example, restorative justice schemes, circles of support and accountability for sex offenders and therapeutic community regimes in prisons).

The key points of peacemaking criminology

- *Peacemaking criminology seeks to challenge the inherent violence involved in the criminal and criminal justice process*
- *Peacemaking criminologists reject the hierarchical, violent and harmful nature of much criminology, and attempt to isolate, identify and subdue offenders through oppressive practices*
- *Peacemaking criminologists reject the notion of solving harms by inflicting harms, and seek a more socially just criminal justice system, particularly promoting inclusion, by attempting to bring people together collectively*
- *Peacemaking criminology has been criticised however. It is perhaps not so much a criminological theory as an attitude or viewpoint, others have suggested as an ideology it is one associated with privilege and lack of understanding of the realities of the world. Similarly, many criminologists would not consider themselves as 'peacemaking', and it is perhaps a term that is more appropriate for some specific works by criminologists rather than a term used to describe the authors more generally.*

Cultural criminology

Examples: Katz (1988); Ferrell and Saunders (1995)

Cultural criminology is often regarded as *the* emerging theoretical concept. Its origins can be contested, and are drawn from a range of theoretical traditions such as those of the Chicago School and 'interactionist criminology' and the work of the Birmingham Centre for Contemporary

Cultural Studies in the 1970s. Cultural criminology examines subculture, style and meaning. Cultural criminology in its most extreme promotes the formulation of a criminological *verstenhen* where the researcher attempts to understand (perhaps even sympathetically) the emotions and meanings that are associated with crime and crime control (Ferrell, 2001).

What Katz proposed was a shift in thinking about the act of crime. He raised questions about the lived experience of crime – its adrenaline, its pleasure, its visual impact and feeling. His work can perhaps be considered as the starting point for a 'cultural criminology' which now tends to ask questions about what it is to be involved in criminality in terms of emotion and feeling. Continuing in this trend, Jeff Ferrell and Clinton Sanders' edited collection *Cultural Criminology* (1995) is more commonly recognised for coining the term.

Cultural criminology takes its lead from the growth in 'cultural studies' as a separate area of academic inquiry. The subject matter for cultural studies draws upon a range of theoretical concepts that ranges from feminism to film studies. In terms of criminology this has broadened the focus of academic inquiry. Ferrell and Saunders captured the essence of the ethos of 'cultural criminology' stressing the link between popular culture, style and criminality. They argued that 'the collective practice of criminality and the criminalisation of everyday life...are cultural enterprises' (1995: 7).

Cultural criminology is a fairly new addition to criminological theory, and therefore is perhaps unlikely at this time to appear in criminology textbooks as a separate branch of thought, although it is gaining momentum and has some stanch. That stated, there have already been some critics. Katz's (1988) work has been criticised by both the political right (who regard his work as too concerned with the criminal's point of view) and left (for irresponsibility in celebrating the hedonistic nature of crime).

The key points of cultural criminology

- *At its most basic level, 'cultural criminology' draws its influence from 'cultural studies' and imports the insights of cultural studies into criminology*
- *Cultural criminology is associated with subcultural studies and ethnography, along with research methods drawn from cultural studies such as media and cultural analysis, or a combination of these methods*
- *Cultural criminologists regard crime as a shared and collective experience involving symbols and meanings, collective ideas and identity, human communication and interaction, emotion and feelings*
- *Much cultural criminology is in almost direct opposition to administrative, positivistic and realist criminology.*

> ***Common pitfall:*** While it is important to acknowledge the recent emergence of a school of cultural criminology, it should be remembered that much early criminology, including much left idealism and conflict criminology, was the product of cultural studies and cultural analysis.

Journalism and offender accounts

Examples: Morrison (1998); Campbell (1993); James (2003)

Some of the most interesting accounts of the criminal justice system come not from academics but from those who have offended. Similarly some of the most controversial and debated texts published in recent years have not come from the pens of 'academic' criminologists but instead have been penned by journalists. Blake Morrison's *As If* documents the circumstances surrounding the murder of James Bulger in Liverpool in 1993 and the subsequent trial of the two killers, who were themselves children. In a similar study, Gita Sereny's *The Case of Mary Bell* and follow up *Cries Unheard* examined the life of ten-year-old murderer Mary Bell who killed two little boys aged three and four in 1968. Indeed what constitutes criminology perhaps should not be narrowly defined and restricted to academic studies because by doing so we perhaps exclude some of the most popular and controversial discussions of crime. *The Case of Mary Bell, Cries Unheard* and *As If* all sparked controversy upon publication, stirred a large amount of discussion, and had an audience that is much greater and more significant in terms of promoting debate than a great many 'academic texts'. However, there exists a problem in separating those sources useful to criminologists into neat categories, and journalism is a case in point. What separates journalistic work from pure 'true crime' and non-fiction writing?

Perhaps it is driven by a more inquiring and questioning philosophy, but it can be hard to tell. There exists an array of texts that criminologists can draw upon, and so long as criminologists are reserved and critical of the material that they encounter, there is no reason that 'academic' texts alone be considered the subject matter of criminology. The more considered writing that tends to appear in 'broadsheet' newspapers (the *Guardian, Times, Independent,* the *Telegraph* etc.) is often used by criminologists (although they tend to avoid tabloid newspapers such as the *Sun,* the *Mirror, The Daily Mail* etc.). Those studying academic courses in criminology may find much that is of worth in the former in terms of debates about crime, the latter are perhaps better avoided.

The key points on journalism and offender accounts

- *New journalism is used to describe a style of writing that involves self-reflection combined with investigative journalism, and therefore stands apart from 'opinion-based work' of books that provide more voyeuristic insights into 'true crime'*
- *It has been argued that criminologists must recognise the multiple influences that they can, and do, draw upon – these often involve contributions from those who would not consider themselves criminologists*
- *Accounts written by those that have been involved within the criminal justice system (most notably offender's accounts) can be extremely useful in terms of furthering knowledge and gaining insight.*

❝ Influential criminologists Sir Leon Radzinowicz expressed a concern with the divide between criminological theory and policy and practice in Britain: 'What I find profoundly disturbing is the gap between criminology and criminal policy' (1999: 469). Do you think his appraisal is correct with regard to contemporary criminological theory? ❞

While Radzinowicz is quoted a little out of context, the argument that criminological theory has less influence upon contemporary debate is one that could be fiercely contested. Three strands of theory have proved extremely influential in recent years in Britain: right realism, left realism and administrative criminology. I would expect a good student to know about these theories, to be able to summarise them, but also to be able to demonstrate how they have influenced policy development; for example, administrative criminology has links to situational crime prevention, right realism has influenced the development of 'zero tolerance' styles of policing.

Taking it **FURTHER**

I have called this chapter 'Contemporary criminology' because it intends to highlight some of criminology's emerging theoretical positions. That stated, what in criminology counts as contemporary is changeable, and new insights and contributions are always emerging. The best way to stay aware of developments in criminology is through journals: the *British Journal of Criminology, Theoretical Criminology, The European Journal of Criminology* and *The Howard Journal of Criminal Justice* are all valuable and should not be overlooked as sources of information, with a number offering favourable subscription rates to students. Similarly, the Centre for Crime and Justice Studies, at Kings College, London offers discount joining rates to students. Members receive the centre's magazine *Criminal Justice Matters*, a quarterly publication (each on a specific theme) that blends theoretical academic criminology with practice issues, and will assist in maintaining awareness of contemporary concerns within criminology.

Textbook guide

Much of the work by core thinkers highlighted above is available in McLaughlin et al.'s *Criminological Perspectives* (2003), which really ought to be considered a must-buy book for any undergraduate criminology student. Katherine Williams' (2004) *Textbook on Criminology* is now in its fifth edition and is extremely up to date.

2.6	
crime statistics and crime data	

Core areas: **The development of crime statistics**
Primary and secondary data in criminology
Recorded crime and official statistics
Crime 'clear up' rates
The advantages of using official statistics
'Measuring the dark figure': The British Crime Survey; Local crime surveys; Feminist victim surveys
Problems with statistics
Politics and crime statistics

Running themes

Crime statistics and crime data are one of the sources which have been used by a wide number of criminologists from a range of perspectives, yet as the **research methods** that inform their collection, they have been much criticised. Crime statistics have a **practical application** and can influence both policy and practice in the criminal justice system. Whilst they can present a picture of rates of crime and victimisation, they also **discriminate** against some groups. Much of the problem with crime statistics arises out of concerns about **evidence** (in terms of how accurate a picture of crime they can give us). Do they present an accurate **representation** of the people's experiences or levels of crime or the amount of crime in society?

Key thinkers

Adolphe Quetelet (1796–1874) was a Belgian astronomer who came across the first French crime statistics whilst working in Paris. After noticing that deaths year on year was consistent, he suggested that correlations in this social data were similar to those consistencies found in astronomy. As Quetelet studied crime statistics in greater detail, he formed the opinion that some people were disproportionately more likely to commit crime than others; these people tended to be young, male, poor, unemployed and under-educated. Quetelet eventually suggested that propensity to engage in crime was due to moral character, and that instilling 'rational and temperate habits, more regulated passions and foresight' would prevent crime. The logical solution to him lay in enhancing 'moral education', improving social conditions and increasing the quality of individuals' lives. Crime was not freely chosen but was dependant upon and even created by society.

Trevor Jones, Brian MacLean and Jock Young (a group of 'left realist' criminologists) conducted a victimisation survey in 1986 known as *The Islington Crime Survey*. This study found that the levels of crime for Islington (an inner city London area experiencing high levels of poverty) were much higher than those generally found by the British Crime Survey. They argued that crime was a problem that disproportionately effected poorer communities and marginalised groups including women and ethnic minorities. This study served to facilitate the development of left realist criminology and the associated concept of relative deprivation.

The development of crime statistics

Crime statistics are essentially one of the criminologist's main tools in investigating 'crime levels', 'patterns of crime' and 'crime trends'. As a subject, criminology is reliant upon evidence, and crime statistics of data is often the basis of criminological theory. The government in France in 1827 published the first crime statistics. It was shortly after this that Andre-Michel Guerry (1802–66) and Adolphe Quetelet (see above) published perhaps what could be regarded as the first works of scientific criminology by using these statistics. This began a trend of positivistic criminology that attempted to make assertions about crime based upon statistical information.

Primary and secondary data in criminology

To recap from Chapter 2.2 on research methods, social scientists interpret those terms in a manner that is different to historians. Primary data to the social scientist is data that they themselves have collected. A variety of different research methods may have been used to collect this data, for example interviews, questionnaires and observations. A secondary source is information that has been produced by someone else, but a social scientist uses for his or her own purposes. Secondary sources will therefore contain any biases or faults that were built into the original work. This is extremely important when we look at criminological work that is based upon crime statistics, as bias or inaccuracy built into data collection will impact upon findings.

Crime statistics have a political application, they are used by people, often to further or support their arguments and assertions. Crime statistics can be abused, and are always open to interpretation. You must ask questions whenever someone attempts to make claims that they suggest are supported or even 'proved' by crime statistics.

Recorded crime and official statistics

Each year the Home Office and various other governmental departments will produce a mass of statistics, many of which are potentially valuable to criminologists. The most obvious example of this data for the criminologist is criminal statistics, but others including prison statistics and social trends are also of great use. These statistics can now be accessed fairly easily through the internet, and you might be well advised to familiarise yourself with some of this information. In England and Wales, official crime data gathered from police and court records dates back to 1876, and despite warnings to the contrary, have also long been treated as an accurate measure of crime (especially by both the media and politicians). Official crime statistics essentially deal with all recorded crime (generated through police records).

There are a number of problems with this information however; perhaps the obvious starting point is with the victim reporting the crime, which we know to be one of the core problems with official crime statistics. As official statistics only record *reported* crime, the victim must decide to report the crime to the police if the crime is to be recorded. There may be a number of instant barriers that prevent this from happening: The belief that police won't be able to do anything; the victim regarding the matter too trivial; fearing the consequences of reporting; not wanting to get involved with the police; a lack of respect for the police; or feeling embarrassed or ashamed. It is estimated that there is a massive under-reporting of crime. Anything up to 50% of crime is therefore not evident in official crime statistics. Criminologists term this unreported crime 'the dark figure'.

If the victim *does* contact the police, there is still no guarantee that the crime will be recorded. The police have to decide whether what is reported to them amounts to a crime, and it may be that what the victim regards as an offence, the police will not view as a breach of the criminal law. If that were to be the case, the police would not record the incident. If the police believe that a crime has been committed, the police then have to decide if it is a 'notifiable offence'. The meaning of this term and the crimes that it covers are detailed in the rules regarding which crimes are counted, produced by the Home Office.

The crimes that are recorded can change and vary. Clearly such changes do raise questions about what general inferences can be made about accurately comparing levels of crime and crime trends for different times.

> *Many introductory criminology and criminal justice courses contain assessment and exam questions on crime statistics and crime data, with questions about the reliability of official crime statistics commonplace. Remember such questions almost naturally lend themselves to critical analysis (see Part 3).*

Crime 'clear up' rates

Included in official crime statistics are details of how many crimes are 'cleared up' and details of the number of people that are 'preceded against', however, here again official statistics can only give a partial picture. The Home Office governs the rules regarding the circumstances in which a crime can be regarded as cleared up. The most common refers to when a person has been 'proceeded against' for an offence, which means that some type of formal action has been taken, for example, the perpetrator has received a police caution. However this also includes being taken to court but not subsequently convicted. A crime can also be regarded as cleared up if a court takes it into consideration (essentially if the individual admits the offence but is not sentenced specifically for it). Crimes can also be regarded as cleared up if the individual admits the offence but it is thought that there would be no useful purpose in prosecuting that individual.

Common pitfall: Do not take 'proceeded against' to mean that the crime has necessarily been solved, as this is not the case.

It is this that in the past has caused a great deal of controversy, in particular relating to a police practice known as 'cuffing' where known offenders, often already in prison, helped the police to improve clear up rates by admitting to crimes that they had not committed or had no knowledge of.

That stated, clear up rates overall are very low: The 2003/4 crime statistics showed that the proportion of recorded crimes that were detected through an offender being charged or summoned, cautioned, having an offence taken into consideration or receiving a fixed penalty notice was just 18.8%, a fall from nearer 50% in the 1960s. However, there are also large differences in the clear up rates between different types of crime; with the most serious categories of crime generally having the higher clear up rates than property offences.

The advantages of using official crime statistics

Whilst there are clearly limitations in using crime statistics, criminologists generally tend to highlight the problems, and not address some of the benefits of statistics. The principal benefit of crime statistics has to be that if one isn't going to use crime statistics to make inferences about the extent of crime in society, what else can they use? The answer is that there is little. Both official crime statistics and the British Crime Survey are well resourced, and there would be little opportunity for independent researchers to undertake such extensive analysis. The government routinely collects data that researchers would otherwise undoubtedly find it difficult to access. Similarly the ethical complexities involved in the research process generally are removed when a researcher uses secondary data, such as crime statistics. If the researcher recognises the bias and problems that are recognised, crime statistics can provide at the least a useful starting point for criminologists.

> *Although crime statistics are often heavily criticised, there is certainly an argument to be made for the usefulness of this data. We must ask ourselves, if we totally discredit crime statistics, as a means of knowing about the extent of crime, is there an alternative source that could tell us more?*

'Measuring the dark figure'

The British Crime Survey (BCS)

During the 1960s, the 'dark figure of crime' ignored by official statistics came to be scrutinised by a number of American studies. Experimental surveys were carried out with random samples, where households were asked whether anyone in that property had been the victim of crime within the previous year, and whether this offence had been reported to the police. These surveys are now referred to by criminologists as 'victim surveys', with the best known of these being the official British Crime Survey (BCS). The BCS is now conducted annually, with a sample of 40,000 and the results published (alongside the official crime statistics) by the Home Office. The survey is now cited as a much more reliable picture of the true extent of crime than police statistics, because it asks a random section of the population about their experience of crime in the previous 12 months, and therefore bypasses some of the criticisms of official statistics stemming from the problems with recording crime. The complex sampling procedure employed by the BCS aims to produce a representative picture of cross sections of all private households in England and Wales, and all individuals aged 16 or over living in them.

However there are a number of problems with the BCS. As it draws evidence from the public, it is somewhat subjective, and the crimes that are reported are not always easily classifiable (which makes comparisons with police records difficult). As it only surveys households it makes no mention of crimes committed against business premises (commercial burglaries, shop thefts) and excludes homeless people, who are victims of a disproportionate amount of crime. Similarly the exclusion of those under 16 may also lead to exclusion of some types of offence (robberies involving mobile phones are most prevalent amongst young people). As the individual needs to know that they were a victim, it can also miss complex frauds and what criminologists term corporate and white-collar crime. There have also been a number of questions raised regarding the accuracy of self-reporting, with the potential for exaggeration, forgetfulness, unwillingness to disclose, and misunderstanding, all potentially serving as limiting factors. That stated, despite potential limitations, the BCS is regarded by many criminologists as a much more accurate picture than that provided by official statistics.

Local crime surveys

Whilst the British Crime Survey is now regarded as presenting a much more accurate picture of the extent of crime than official statistics, it tells little of the specific geography of crime. In particular it allows little insight into the experiences of urban 'high crime' estates. This factor was recognised by left realist criminologists, who emerged in the 1980s, and argued that rises in crime were real, and were felt most by those in deprived inner city estates.

A number of criminologists of the left realist school decided to study crime in specific areas, and sought to use victim surveys to explore the experience of crime in both Merseyside (Kingsley, 1985) and Islington (Jones, McLean and Young, 1986). In particular these studies supported the assertions of their authors regarding the damaging effects of crime on particularly poor neighbourhoods, and displayed much higher levels of crime than official statistics. The studies were not without problems with regard their research methods, but highlighted a number of features previously not seen in official studies.

Feminist victim surveys

Whilst the studies undertaken in Merseyside and Islington are somewhat different to the BCS, in that they attempted to present a less distorted picture of crime, and the left realists made advances in documenting the lived experiences of some marginalised groups, the picture presented would be distorted if the achievement were to be credited to them alone. In the 1980s, the desire to learn more about the lived experiences of crime for the very poor, ethnic minorities and women influenced left leaning local authorities to fund research experiences. Whilst that helped the left realist causes, it also allowed feminist criminologists to begin to investigate women's experiences of crime, and re-enforced the stark reality that it is 'the home that is the place where women are most likely to be sexually or physically assaulted' (Stanko, 1998: 41). This point was perhaps made most starkly by Hammer and Saunders (1984) who interviewed 129 women in Leeds to gain insight into their experiences of crime. They found that 59% of the sample had experienced either sexual harassment, the threat of sexual violence or actual sexual violence within the previous 12 months. They also found that there were four reported cases of serious sexual assault, which was more than the 1982 BCS found in some 11,000 interviews!

Problems with statistics

As illustrated above, crime statistics can often throw up a range of findings that are quite frankly inaccurate and unrepresentative, here are some more examples:

- Victimisation studies often show grossly low levels of serious interpersonal crime, such as the 1982 BCS which found only one attempted rape, a figure which for 11,000 interviews is simply nonsense.

- Self-report studies often display little variation in terms of juvenile delinquency between class and race, and considerably less variation between gender than can be expected. This has lead some criminologists to suggest that there is no relationship between class and crime, a claim that again may not be the case in reality.

- The National Crime Victimisation Survey (NCVS) in America, has often shown white men to have a similar or greater likelihood of being assaulted than black men, which runs in total contradiction to homicide rates and other statistical evidence.

- The International Crime and Victimisation Survey (ICVS) frequently reports rates of violence that are in total contradiction to homicide rates.

Politics and crime statistics

With each annual publication of the crime statistics, there will be an accompanying debate in broadsheet newspapers that can be extremely interesting. Editorials in broadsheet newspapers can provide insightful comment on what inferences crime statistics allow us to make, and these are usually accompanied by comment from the leading political parties.

Common pitfall: Crime and crime control is often a political business, and you should remember that while statistics are not necessarily politically driven, those who collect and use them may be. You should always approach statistical research with some caution, and be very careful not to fall into the trap of making arguments along the lines of 'The British Crime Surveys show that it is a fact that violent crime is rising'.

" How reliable are official crime statistics? "

This essay really lends itself to using the advantages and disadvantages method in Chapter 3.5 but remember to blend in some contemporary examples of the political debate that surrounds crime statistics. A good answer would display knowledge of the academic debate surrounding the use of official crime statistics. Mentioning Adolphe Quetelet and discussing the history of crime statistics' development in brief could provide an opening for your answer, but don't neglect contemporary works (see the Textbook guide opposite). Remember to be critical in your analysis, and credit both the positives and negatives associated with official crime statistics. Also remember that you should try to reach a conclusion.

Taking it ***FURTHER***

It is well worth remembering that Quetelet began writing on crime far earlier than Lombroso, but is not credited as the founding father of criminology. One of his assertions was that 'The Crimes which are annually committed seem to be a necessary result of our social organisation...Society prepares the crime, and the guilty are only the instruments by which it is executed'. In essence, Quetelet was arguing that the causation of crime was not the individual, but features in society. It is therefore perhaps not surprising that politically, both Beccarias' notion of 'freewill' and Lombroso's argument that the cause of crime was within the individual, found more lasting political influence. Recently there has been a great deal of criticism made of official crime statistics in books and journals by cultural criminologists (see as an example, Young, 2003) who have been very critical of administrative, positivistic criminology, and especially critical of statistical information.

Textbook guide

There are a number of good textbooks that can provide further insight into discussion of crime statistics. I would not hesitate to recommend Coleman and Moynihan's (1996) *Understanding Crime Data: Haunted by the Dark Figure*. Similarly Mike Maguire's (2002) chapter 'Crime statistics: the data explosion and its implications' in *The Oxford Handbook of Criminology* is extremely good, while Mayhew (2000) offers a comprehensive overview of victim surveys; local, national and international. There is a large amount of statistical information about crime now available on the internet: In Britain, the Home Office Research and Statistics Directorate website can be accessed through www.homeoffice.gov.uk, which also includes a link to the most recent British Crime Survey.

2.7	
crime and the media	

Core areas: **Introduction**

Media coverage of crime

The media and the fear of crime

Media news values

Theorising the media and crime: Deviancy amplification; The moral panic

Re-thinking moral panics

Positive media representation?

Running themes

Criminological discussion about the media tends to stress the **power** of the media, and its ability to **discriminate** and promote **inequality**. The media **representation** of crime is undoubtedly a very **political** process, which is driven by different **political** and **economic** motives, which can impact upon public thinking about crime and influence political decisions.

Key thinkers

Leslie Wilkins introduced the concept of 'deviancy amplification' in his work *Social Deviancy* (1964). Essentially this idea describes a process where media, state and public reactions to non-conforming or deviant acts serve not to control the level of deviancy, but actually increase it. Wilkins' concept links with integrationist criminology and labelling theories.

Stan Cohen first published *Folk Devils and Moral Panics* in 1972 – a book which fits with the concepts of integrationist criminologists. In it Cohen examines the construction of the 'Mods and Rockers' and introduced the notion of the 'moral panic'. The term 'moral panic' is one much used in sociology and criminology and still has contemporary relevance (examples include paedophiles, joy-riders, football hooligans and mobile phone muggers) and it is vital to be familiar with Cohen's argument when debating media representation of crime.

Media coverage of crime

Before we begin to look at just how the media uses crime, it may be valuable to consider how, when and why the media selects stories. Most media institutions seek to attract as wide an audience as possible to maximise their profits, and even media that is not profit driven has to compete with other forms that are for an audience. To attract and retain audiences media products have to entertain, be dramatic or exciting, and sometimes cause outright shock. It is on this basis that stories and features are selected by all forms of media. As crime is shocking, entertaining, dramatic and exciting, it is unsurprising that the media often chooses to use crime.

> *In order to comment upon the media and crime, it is vital that you have knowledge of current issues and debates. To this end it is well worth reading both broadsheet and tabloid newspapers, and watching the media. It is also important to question what you are told by the media, for example ask yourself 'Why is that headline being used?', 'Why is this news story appearing now?', 'Who is setting the agenda?', 'Whose opinion am I hearing?' and 'Is there another side to this argument?'*

Studies into the media's use of crime would seemingly support the assertion that 'crime sells'. In 1989, in a study in the UK, a survey of ten national daily newspapers for four weeks between June and July found that, on average, 12.7% of event-orientated reports were about crime (although there was a great deal of disparity between tabloid and broadsheet newspapers). If you conduct your own survey of either tabloid or broadsheet newspapers you will find that crime is a stable part of their reporting, as it is on television news. However, the types of crime that are reported are not representative. The crimes that are reported are shocking and alarming; murder, rape and serious violence. This can tend to convey the impression that such crimes are not rare (which they are) but are frequent, thereby creating an unrepresentative picture of the extent and type of crime prevalent in society.

The media and the fear of crime

Crime is seemingly a troubling aspect of life. That is perhaps unsurprising given that the word crime generally evokes a fear of the most serious criminal acts (murder, rape, serious violent assault). Yet these acts are relatively uncommon, whilst in reality we need to confront the possibility that many of those who commit offences are not that different to 'us'. Crime is not uncommon, but often it is not that extreme in nature.

However, fear of crime amongst the British is seemingly high. For criminologists an important issue is the public perception of the risk of crime, or 'the fear of crime'. The media is likely to play a central role in creating public perceptions of crime and therefore influencing their perceptions about the extent of crime and the risk of suffering it.

Media news values

So how might the media contribute to society's understanding and perception of crime? A number of reasons have been suggested but there are perhaps two considerations that over-ride all others:

1. **News value** – Events must meet a required level of significance to be perceived as 'news-worthy' that will differ according to the news medium (for example, whether the news medium is regional or national), and the location of the story (for example, a British serial killer who kills five people will receive considerably more attention than a large scale humanitarian disaster in a third world country). Similarly, once a story makes the press, it must continue to have an impact, something 'fresh'. As the process of criminal investigation and prosecution can be timely, some stories may disappear only to be re-discovered at a later point (the murder trial at crown court some months later for example).

2 **Impact** – The stories selected by the media are chosen for their impact. An element of shock may be enough, but essentially the main consideration is how the story will engage the audience. News editors will select stories that are sensational, with embellished descriptions. It is these stories that also seemingly have a large impact upon the public. Similarly if the event is one which can generate a large swell of public sympathy, it will quickly be seized upon, for example, particularly violent physical assaults and robberies of the elderly are often lead stories in regional news mediums. The crimes that receive the most attention are the crimes that happen least frequently, but are most shocking. Examples are the murders of James Bulger by two young boys, or the murder of Holly Wells and Jessica Chapman. Such crimes are extremely rare when compared to high frequency but less serious crimes that are unlikely to ever be reported in the media.

Highly graphic violent crime stories that contain sensational headlines not only seemingly have a massive receptive audience in the form of the general public, they also have an impact upon policy and practice in the criminal justice system. For example, the murder of James Bulger, mentioned above, is seen by a number of academics as kick-starting an unrelenting rise in the use of imprisonment. It also helped to overcome civil liberty arguments against the spread of CCTV, and was also influential in leading to the change in the common law presumption of 'doli incapax', which presumed that children below the age of 14 did not know the difference between right and wrong – this then led to a change in the age of criminal responsibility in the UK being changed to ten.

But to see the media's role in creating a fear of crime solely through its reporting of 'real' crime is perhaps to under-estimate the types of media that influence public opinion. Crime and the criminal justice system is a fascinating subject that interests a large number of people; yet is also shrouded in mystery. Crime contains all the ingredients required to produce entertaining drama. It provides so much material for both fact and fiction accounts that are meant to entertain us, from novels to magazines, documentaries to soap operas. To suggest that the public are influenced only by the news media is perhaps to under-estimate the way that popular culture can impact upon public perception.

Theorising the media and crime

Much discussion of the media's impact has been linked to integrationist criminology, for example, the media's role in labelling 'deviant' or criminal behaviours. When thinking about the way in which the media portrays crime, there are two theories which have remained extremely influential: deviancy amplification and moral panic.

There are two theorists who are synonymous with criminological theory linked to the media, both of whom have contributed primary criminological theories that seek to link the media with crime directly. These theories go some way toward addressing the way in which the media can understand the media's influence on the criminal justice process.

Deviancy amplification

British Criminologist Leslie Wilkins' concept of 'deviancy amplification' was developed and emerged at the height of the influence of interactionist criminology and 'labelling theories'. Wilkins suggested that deviancy amplification is a process whereby the media, police, public and political reaction to non-conformist behaviour acts not to control deviant behaviour, but has an opposite effect of increasing it. Wilkins used the term to explore the relationship between levels of tolerance and intolerance and the re-enforcement of deviant identity. He suggested that in societies where there were intolerant responses to deviance, more acts were criminalised and more action taken against criminals. He suggested that this would increasingly lead to the isolation and alienation of groups who would therefore commit more crime, and be rejected more vehemently by wider society. As a result, a perpetuating cycle or 'positive feedback loop' would emerge. Wilkins therefore regards effective controls placed upon crime, as increasing the levels of crime. The more effective the controls, the more marginalised the group, the more crime will be resultant. Whilst not empirically testable, the explanation still has some supporters (Silverman and Wilson (2002) draw upon it to explain the contemporary alarm over paedophiles). That said, Wilkins' concept has seemingly been surpassed by a theory that is still commonly used in criminology, that of the moral panic.

Moral panics

In what amounts to one of the seminal studies of criminology, youth, the media and social control, Stan Cohen presented a picture of the inter-relationships in the construction of deviance. Cohen argues that at times of wider social unease, or rapid change, folk devils and moral panics serve to create a sense of control over these events, groups and individuals who would appear to threaten the societal norms. His research was based upon the phenomenon of young people forming groups of 'Mods' and 'Rockers' in the 1960s and particularly their behaviour (which began with minor acts of vandalism and some violence in Clacton in Essex over the May bank holiday weekend of 1964) and the evolving social response that stemmed from this. The press printed over-sensationalised stories of gang violence, and running battles as front-page news. This in turn led to increased policing of these groups, but also served to create a greater sense of being a 'Mod' or a 'Rocker' for young people, which polarised these groups even further. Together, these factors led in turn to more arrests, which served to justify the original reporting. Cohen suggested that there were three essential elements of control culture:

1 **Diffusion** – Which describes the process where events in other places and at other times may be connected to an initial event

2 **Escalation** – Which describes the calls for action to counter a threat, for example, 'We shouldn't have to put up with their behaviour any more' or 'Something should be done'

3 **Innovation** – Which details stronger powers that are granted to the courts or police to deal with the threat, for example, in the case of football hooliganism this could be the football banning order.

For Cohen the media played a central role in publicising the activities of the groups, and causing an accompanying uneasiness. He suggested that the media shape debate by providing further information, which then serves to re-enforce the original reports.

The problems with the concept of the moral panic

In considering the role the media plays in socially constructing the public perception of crime and deviance, the moral panic thesis may be a useful one, but problems with it remain, for example:

- Not all 'folk devils' can be said to be vulnerable, or unfairly marginalised. Jewkes (2004: 76) gives paedophiles as one such example, however other accounts see this group as 'demonised' and subject to a moral panic (Silverman and Wilson, 2002)
- The concept of the 'moral panic' fails to ask adequate questions about the initial causation of deviant behaviour, the term deviancy attests to similarities

between behaviours that are often different (is the fear of paedophiles comparable to the fear of recreational ecstasy use by young people?)

- According to Cohen's own testimony, moral panics should be short lived, however, there is some evidence that continual anxiety exists with regard some forms of 'deviant behaviour'
- There is a difficulty with the term morality. Morality can imply a consensus view within society, whilst this may be true in some instances, other morals are not shared throughout society. Similarly we encounter problems when we consider that the term moral panic appears to have spread to embrace panics that contain 'little or no moral element' (Jewkes, 2004: 78)
- Some accounts tend to see the moral panic as a tool of the politically elite, where they cynically manipulate both the media and the public, whilst others see them as generated by the public in response to very real fears that exist; these accounts are at odds with each other.

Re-thinking moral panics

It can be easy to fall into the trap of displaying a superficial understanding of the term 'moral panic'. When you use this term, ensure that you are aware of some of criticisms that can be made of it; while the idea might seem convincing, remember there are problems with this term.

It was not just Cohen's arguments that relied upon the notion of the moral panic, indeed the concept was central to Stuart Hall and colleagues' *Policing the Crisis* (1978) which suggested that the media seized upon mugging, and created an authoritarian inspired moral panic. However, critics such as Waddington were extremely dismissive, indeed Waddington noted that contrary to the arguments made by Hall and his associates, 'mugging' was undergoing real rises. He therefore questioned what a 'proportionate' response would be (1986). Taking this theme further there has been a number of accounts that have sought to re-position the notion of the moral panic. Goode and Ben-Yehuda (1994) have argued that the concept of the 'moral panic' needs to be revisited and have suggested that there should be three distinct theories or approaches to the moral panic:

1 **The grassroots model** – Which details the type of panic that is generated bottom up, where, for example, the public expresses a genuinely felt sense of concern about a threat, even if it is mistaken or misguided

2 **The elite engineered approach** – Which is where a group of elites deliberately and consciously promote a concern or fear

3 **The investment-group approach** – Which stems from the rule-makers and legislators, or the moral entrepreneurs who create moral panics in an attempt to create a crusade for greater control.

Goode and Ben-yehuda (1994) also suggest that a moral panic has five core characteristics:

(a) A disproportionate reaction
(b) Concern about a threat
(c) Hostility toward the subject of the panic
(d) A widespread agreement that the threat is a real one
(e) Volatility: Moral panics are random in terms of scale or length.

Positive media representation?

Much of the discourse on the media's representation of crime concerns whether it promotes a fear of crime – far fewer studies have suggested that the media can have a positive effect. Recently this position has been revisited slightly, with some academics even going so far as to suggest that the positive power of fictional portrayals of the criminal justice system can educate the public. For example, Wilson and O'Sullivan (2004) have argued that film and television drama can accurately represent the brutal realities of prison and be used to convey the message of prison reform. This is an interesting emerging debate that promotes the positive potential of media representations rather than accentuating the most negative media portrayals of crime and punishment.

❝ How useful is the concept of the moral panic in terms of examining the public's anxiety about paedophiles? ❞

This question will allow you to examine the notion of the moral panic in some detail, and you should do this. Introduce and describe the concept of moral panic and link it with Cohen's work, but be aware that the question is quite specific and it is necessary to acknowledge two arguments. Yvonne Jewkes suggests paedophiles present a real risk to children and the public may be expressing legitimate concern, while other academics, such as Silverman and Wilson believe the media are cynically exploiting public fears and generating unnecessary alarm. You might want to think which you feel is more likely. Remember, once again, that reading around the subject and having a knowledge of recent events would be beneficial (such as the *News of the World*'s campaign to 'name and shame' sex offenders after the murder of Sarah Payne).

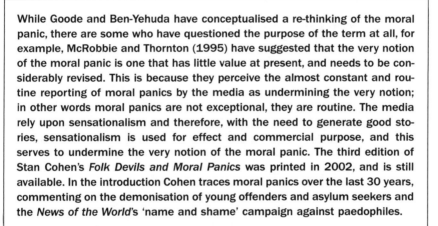

Taking it **FURTHER**

While Goode and Ben-Yehuda have conceptualised a re-thinking of the moral panic, there are some who have questioned the purpose of the term at all, for example, McRobbie and Thornton (1995) have suggested that the very notion of the moral panic is one that has little value at present, and needs to be considerably revised. This is because they perceive the almost constant and routine reporting of moral panics by the media as undermining the very notion; in other words moral panics are not exceptional, they are routine. The media rely upon sensationalism and therefore, with the need to generate good stories, sensationalism is used for effect and commercial purpose, and this serves to undermine the very notion of the moral panic. The third edition of Stan Cohen's *Folk Devils and Moral Panics* was printed in 2002, and is still available. In the introduction Cohen traces moral panics over the last 30 years, commenting on the demonisation of young offenders and asylum seekers and the *News of the World*'s 'name and shame' campaign against paedophiles.

Textbook guide

Yvonne Jewkes' (2004) *Media and Crime* is a good introductory textbook that presents extremely comprehensive coverage of this subject area. John Muncie's chapter in Muncie and Mclaughlin's *The Problem of Crime* (2001) is a useful source, as is Jewkes' chapter in Muncie and Wilson's *Student Handbook of Criminal Justice and Criminology* (2004).

| 2.8 | |
| youth and crime | |

Core areas: **What is the trouble with kid's today?**

America: Chicago and juvenile delinquency

British studies of youth subcultures

Radical non-intervention?

Youth offending

Youths as victims

Running themes

Young people are quite frequently the subject of debate about their criminality, and there is **evidence** to suggest that this is based in part upon **inequality** and **discrimination** – we tend to view youths as problematic, often because of their offending, but little consideration is given to their victimisation. Young people themselves are a group whose voice is unlikely to be heard, and because they are relatively **powerless** in society, they tend to be frequently **represented** in a negative manner. Much criminology has attempted to examine the experiences of young people with this backdrop in mind, but clearly such discussion cannot be separated from interconnected subjects of **race**, **class** and **gender**.

Key thinkers

Edwin M Schur – was a Professor and head of Sociology at New York University. He made a number of significant contributions to criminology, and was influenced by interactionism and labelling philosophies. More specifically as an interaction-ist Schur felt that if applying labels to people exacerbated the problem, the logical conclusion was to minimise criminalisation. In particular, in *Radical Non-intervention* (1973), Schur suggested that the response to juvenile crime was excessive, and that the criminal justice system should 'leave kids alone whenever possible' (1973: 155). Whilst his argument is far from universally accepted, it is perhaps a relevant and interesting concept in the sphere of youth justice.

Geoffrey Pearson – Pearson's *Hooligan: A History of Respectable Fears* (1983) should be a starting point for you in putting contemporary 'adult' concerns about troublesome youth into perspective; both historically and sociologically. Pearson challenged the misconception that there existed a bygone 'golden era' in relation to young people's behaviour, arguing that many contemporary concerns, such as those regarding 'troublesome youth' were not new, but instead formed part of a long established trend. Pearson was a notable figure at the National Deviancy Conference which was associated with the study of evolving youth subculture linked to 'interactionist' criminology (for example, Cohen, 1972; Young, 1971) and he has long promoted the subcultural study of young people (1975).

What's the trouble with kids today?

Fears about youth and criminality are nothing new, indeed, as Pearson has argued there tends to be a perpetual concern regarding young people that is long established (Pearson, 1983). It is also difficult to separate the issue of youth crime into a unique subject area, as we have already seen, the question of youth frequently arises in accounts of the media and it's reporting of crime. That stated, youthful criminality is a long established area of study for criminology. This chapter does not seek to give an overview of the youth justice system, as there are plenty of books that do so, instead it looks specifically at what we know about youth crime, and explanations regarding youthful criminality that criminologists have presented.

Concern with youth, crime and the dangerous classes has not been restricted to contemporary British society; there has been an ever present fear about youth and crime (particularly working class or poor youth and crime). There has been 'Teddy boys', 'Mods', 'Rockers', 'football hooligans', 'skinheads', 'joy-riders' and 'Chavs', the threat of youth crime is never distant – each generation has its dangerous young simply waiting to be discovered. Therefore it is perhaps unsurprising that many of the 'moral panics' we have encountered involve 'youth'.

The concept of the moral panic (see Chapter 2.7) is inseparable from discussions on the topic of youth and crime. You would do well to remember that it is often media portrayals that influence public perceptions of problematic youth.

That stated, youthfulness is certainly a predictor of potential criminality. The peak age of offending for males is 18, whereas for females it is 15, and it is certainly true to suggest that the early onset of criminality is a very good predictor of the likelihood of a continual involvement in crime, as the vast majority of those who go on to be 'persistent' of 'career' criminals start to commit crimes in their early teens. Similarly self-report studies also tend to suggest that offending can be fairly common amongst young people, with the Audit Commission report 'Misspent youth' estimating that the financial cost of youth crime to public services each year was around £1 billion. It has even been suggested that in reality, 'the youth crime problem is the crime problem' (Wilson and Ashton, 2001: 66). However, it is also worth stressing that while an estimated seven million offences are committed by under 18s each year, up to 85% of young offenders cautioned don't come to the attention of the police again within two years, and while there is some disagreement whenever statistics are used, statistics seem to suggest that youth crime may have been falling for some years. It is known that between 1992 and 2001, the number of 10 to 17-year-olds convicted or cautioned fell by 21%.

America: Chicago and Juvenile Delinquency

While in Britain academic inquiry into delinquency and youthful crimi-nality tended to be linked to practical and policy concerns (and biological and psychological positivism) rather than a spirit of social inquiry, in America the agenda was different and enquiry was guided by scholarly endeavour. Particularly from the 1920s, investigations of juvenile crimi-nality tended to stem from the pioneering sociological positivism and the early ethnographic work of the Chicago School of sociology. Therefore American work on youth and crime did not have the same concern with promoting working practices. While sociologists did have a real impact upon political policy, this was perhaps less conscious and deliberate.

The Chicago School:

- *Conducted 'ecological' research which aimed to understand the city of Chicago*
- *Promoted qualitative methods – such as participant observation and life history*
- *Undertook a number of studies with 'delinquent' youths*
- *Promoted theories of social disorganisation and cultural transmission*
- *Proved to be influential in the development of theories such as strain and status frustration*
- *Produced what are now regarded as classic studies of youthful criminality such as Clifford Shaw's* The Jack Roller *(1930).*

Subcultural studies were first used by anthropologists in order to investigate the culture and practices of different societies, but were adapted and used by sociologists from the late 1920s to study social deviance. These studies were widely used by the 1950s in both Britain and America, especially by sociologists studying social deviance and juvenile delinquency, in order to argue that seemingly 'senseless' behaviour of such groups could be understood as a response to the problems that they faced. In both America and Britain, the influence of sociology as an academic discipline helped to promote the social disorganisation theories and interactionist criminology, with attention focused upon youth crime (for some examples see Shaw and McKay, 1942; Cohen, 1955; Cloward and Ohlin, 1960; Sykes and Matza, 1957).

British studies of youth subcultures

It is fair to suggest that in Britain the influence of subcultural studies such as those undertaken by the Chicago school were not influential til some years later, and academic discourse suggests that at this time Britain produced less ethnographic research into juvenile crime than their American counterparts. Perhaps this is partly due to the fact that there seems historically to be some difference in the types of gangs found in Britain and America.

In Britain, John Mays (1954) and David Downes (1966) were the first researchers to investigate youth delinquency in a manner similar to that of Chicago sociologists. Momentum grew, as did studies of youth deviant subcultures, with the work of the Birmingham Centre for Contemporary Cultural Studies. Stuart Hall and Tony Jefferson's (1976) *Resistance Through Rituals* is a classic text that documents well the development of British youth subcultures, while numerous studies of the centre examined some aspects of youthful criminality. Indeed it was the subcultural study of youth that played such a substantial role in promoting interactionist, new deviancy and cultural forms of criminology.

Radical non-intervention?

Criminologists have generated a wealth of evidence on youth and crime, however looking at all the issues that can be gathered together under the banner of youth and crime would not be possible. Therefore I have sought to highlight those theoretical contributions to criminology that either expand our knowledge about young people's behaviour, or provide contributions from theoretical criminologists that might have a wider application and relevance. One such figure is Edwin Schur, an interactionist criminologist who promoted the concept of radical non-intervention. Schur is perhaps one of the most radical criminologists on the subject of youth and crime, arguing that the problems of youthful criminality were actually made worse by the criminal justice system's intervention. His views, produced during the early 1970s stand in stark contrast to those of a great many official, administrative, realist criminologists.

Youth offending

Offending by young people is pretty common. A recent survey found that nearly half of 11 to 16-year-old school children in the UK admit to having broken the law. However, the great majority of young people who commit offences do so infrequently. Similarly the types of crimes committed by young people are rarely that serious, and are usually property crimes such as theft, handling stolen goods, burglary, fraud or forgery and criminal damage, making up more than two-thirds of all youth crime. Despite media attention on violent offending, few cautions or convictions relate to violence. After the peak age of offending, any criminal activity that young people are involved in usually declines, with a particularly sharp decline for criminal damage and violent offences. This is largely thought to be the effect of positive changes in young people's lives, personal and social development: completing education, gaining employment, leaving home and finding a partner can all lead young people away from crime. Where this cannot be said to be the case, however, is when young people have been in custody. The rates of re-offending for those in youth custody are far worse than those for adults. This may not simply be because prison for young people can be an incredibly traumatic and negative experience, but also because the vast majority of young people who appear in prison have experienced incredibly traumatic lives before prison; and this pattern is likely to continue.

Her Majesties Inspectorate of Prisons published a report in 2004 that gives a good example of the multiple traumatic experiences young people in prison face:

Before prison:

- 83% of boys and 65% of girls in prison have previously been excluded from school
- 37% of boys and 43% of girls in prison had previously spent time in care, in a foster home or in both
- 1 in 6 of both boys and girls reported having alcohol problems, and 40% admit having a drug problem

- 12% of boys are fathers, 5% of girls have their own children and a further 3% are pregnant
- Many young people in prison have experienced physical or sexual abuse, and a disproportionate number have mental health problems.

During prison:

- Over one-third of both boys and girls said that they felt unsafe in prison
- 1 in 10 boys and girls admit to being bullied, with 24% of boys and 12% of girls saying they had been physically assaulted
- In 2003, 13 young people killed themselves in custody, there are numerous instances of self-harm amongst young prisoners.

After prison:

- Home office statistics suggest that as many as 75% of young males and 63% of young females will re-offend within two years of their release from custody.

Youths as victims

With some of the above points in mind it is perhaps a point well worth making that concern with youths as potential criminals has not been matched with a recognition or similar level of concern with youths as victims of crime. The perception of youths as troublesome has led to the belief that young people are criminals, rather than being victims. The alarming thing is that this is an inaccurate perception, quite simply because while crime is something associated with youth, so is victimisation.

Youth victimisation

- Over a third (35%) of young people aged 10 to 15 had experienced at least one personal crime in the previous 12 months. This was about the same level as for those aged 16 to 25 (32%) and well above those aged 26 to 65 (14%)
- The types of crime that young people experienced changed with age. Robbery and thefts from the person were less common experiences, for instance, for 10 to 11-year-olds than for 16 to 17-year-olds but other thefts were more common. Differences in the proportion of young people experiencing assaults were not statistically significant but were higher than for those over 21 years

(Continued)

(Continued)

- The degree of repeat victimisation for violent offences was particularly high for young people with 19% of 10 to 15-year-olds experiencing five or more incidents in the previous 12 months
- Offending by young people was the factor most strongly associated with their being victims of personal crime. Other underlying risk factors were the presence of anti-social behaviour in their local area, being male and committing anti-social behaviour
- There was no difference in the level of overall personal crime victimisation between young people in different ethnic groups. Within specific types of crime, white young people were more likely to have been victims of assault than black and minority ethnic young people but were less likely to have been victims of robbery (see Wood, 2005).

❝ In criminology, youth are frequently regarded as perpetrators, but infrequently viewed as victims. Discuss. ❞

You should draw from the theories in this and other chapters to make an argument about the extent to which the representation of youth crime is accurate. Clearly, in many ways, youth is a factor that affects the likelihood of involvement in criminality, but our perception also comes from elsewhere. Remember that the concept of the moral panic might be useful in answering this question because it is possible to argue that our concern with youth crime stems from unjust portrayals in the media.

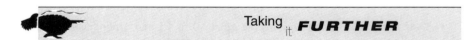

Taking it **FURTHER**

As the subject of this book is 'theoretical criminology' rather than a more general analysis of the criminal justice system, this chapter has offered very little by means of introducing the specific differences in the treatment of young offenders. Roger Smith's *Youth Justice: Ideas, Policy, Practice* is a comprehensive, up to date and critical overview of the youth justice system which students will find useful. As a general overview students should consider reading Tim Newburn's (2002) *Young People, Crime and Youth Justice*. This provides an excellent overview of the subject in a compact form and should be considered essential reading to accompany this chapter.

Textbook guide

These who are new to criminology and want to expand their understanding of this area would be well advised to start with John Muncie's excellent *Youth and Crime*, 2nd edn (2004) now in its second edition. Similarly Brown's (1998) *Understanding Youth and Crime* is a good introductory text.

2.9	
gender and crime	

Core areas: **What do we mean by gender?**

Feminist criminology

Criminology and women

Masculinities and crime

Crime as 'doing masculinity'

Running themes

Clearly the subject of gender and crime is motivated by a desire to examine gender **inequality**, and therefore examine **power** relationships that characterise society, largely with a view to challenging **discrimination**. More recently feminist scholars have highlighted the need to also consider **race** and **class** along with **sex and gender** motivated by an ideology that seeks to promote a socially just society.

Key thinkers

Freda Adler is best known for *Sisters in Crime* (1975). Adler argued that the women's empowerment, as a result of the feminist movement during the 1970s, coincided with a dramatic rise in women's criminal activity. While women had made progress in the legal economy, 'a similar number of determined women have forced their way into the world of major crime such as white collar crime, murder and robbery'. It would be fair to suggest that Adler's theory proved controversial with other feminists. Carol Smart suggested that Adler had fallen victim to 'statistical illusions' (Smart, 1979) and as Pat Carlen suggested, Adler's new female criminal was a continuation of the 'maladjusted masculinity female' of traditional criminology, rejecting her proper feminine role (1983: 376–7).

James Messerschmidt who wrote *Masculinities and Crime* (1993), applied the concepts of 'hegemonic masculinity' to crime (the former being developed by sociologist Robert Connell who in turn was inspired by sociologist Gramsci). Hegemonic masculinity suggests that at any one point in time, there is a dominant form of masculinity (hegemonic masculinity) that subordinates all other forms of masculinity and femininity. Messerschmidt argued that many men's crimes are best understood as a means of 'doing gender' and making masculinity. Messerschmidt suggested that an understanding of various masculinities is central to developing an understanding of crime.

What do we mean by gender?

Before I go any further with this chapter it is important to clarify some of the terms that are used. In this chapter I talk about both sex and gender, and both sex and gender are 'running themes' which you should keep in mind while you study the subject, however it is important that you are clear on what is meant by these terms.

> *Sex is a biological category and gender is a social construction, by this we mean that gender is different to sex. When we use the term sex, we talk about something which is biological and relatively fixed; when we talk about gender we accept social influences.*

In order to demonstrate that gender differences *can* be explained by biology we would have to demonstrate that a substantial or universal difference between men's and women's roles exists across all societies and cultures, at all times and in all places. We would have to show that across all societies men adhere to one set of behaviours and women to another. Further, we would have to show that this difference could be attributed to biology rather than to different modes of upbringing. We know, however, that in many respects, women across time and cultures have inhabited many different worlds, so it is very difficult to sustain a view that biology is the reason for all differences between sexes and in gender roles.

> *Common pitfall:* Many students tend to get confused when it comes to sex
> and gender and what the terms mean. It is important that you are clear about these
> terms.

Feminist criminology

As you will now be aware there isn't a single 'feminist criminology' (see
Chapter 2.4). Feminism tends to be associated with different theoretical perspectives. However, the divisions between feminist criminology can be confusing, and at times serve to detract from the common concern of feminist
thought, which shares some key traits regardless of the perspective it takes.

> *All feminist criminology:*
>
> • *Looks to highlight discrimination against women*
> • *Is concerned by male violence and oppression at both individual and societal levels*
> • *Focuses upon the unequal position of women in society, the victimisation of women
>   and women's victimisation (including that perpetrated by the criminal justice system).*

Liberal feminism

In criminology, liberal feminist work tends to assume that men and
women are essentially the same, shunning notions of biological difference. It sought to highlight the inequitable treatment of women and
girls in the criminal justice system, and suggested that women were
denied the opportunities that men were presented with, which included
the opportunity to commit crime. Perhaps the greatest contribution of
liberal feminism in criminology was the highlighting of the false claim
criminology made of being gender-neutral, when the reality was that
much criminology was gender-blind or based upon biological assumptions supported by no real evidence.

Radical feminism

Radical feminism advocated a more radical response to the experience of
oppression that women encountered from both individual men and 'in
social structures'. It sought to analyse woman's oppression and the structures

that maintained it, but particularly focused upon 'violence against women', 'sexual violence' and 'gender violence' as key strategies that are used to control women. Radical feminists also highlight the patriarchy of the criminal justice system. It has been influential in terms of activism that promoted organisations such as Women's Aid, the rape crisis federation. Radical feminism, as its name conveys, is more radical than liberal feminism, and aims to look at broader themes than individual oppression, instead seeking to understand the wider social circumstances that contribute to perceptions and understanding of crime. Therefore it is less concerned with individual experiences of oppression, and more concerned with the social conditions and structures that contribute to women's oppression.

Socialist feminism

Socialist feminism regards women's oppression as rooted in patriarchal capitalism, and argues that it is essential to consider the interplay between gender and class in order to understand crime. This position has been associated with male criminologists who declare themselves 'pro-feminist'. It occupies a different position from radical feminism insofar as it acknowledges the fact that much 'liberal feminism' ignored issues of class. Rather than regarding 'patriarchy' or men generally as the root cause of women's oppression, it predominantly looks toward capitalism to explain women's oppression.

Criminology and women

Lombroso recognised that women are 'much less criminal than men' in general, and reasoned that this was due to women's unique biology. His work *The Female Offender* written with William Ferrero claimed that women's lesser criminality was explained by their 'piety, maternity, and want of passion, sexual coldness, weakness and underdeveloped intelligence' (1895: 151). Early Marxist criminologist Wilhelm Bonger suggested that 'the average woman of our time has less strength and courage than the average man, and consequently, commits on average fewer crimes than he' (1916: 472) whilst Otto Pollack (1950) is famous for his argument that women were biologically the 'weaker sex'. He asserted that women's criminality was potentially equal to that of men, however, women's ability to 'mask' their criminality (because of a deviousness that resulted from hiding menstruation and faking orgasm) meant that they were more likely to commit crimes typified by deceitfulness and concealment – such as thefts, shoplifting, and perjury. He also, however, argued that women could be influenced by men and were often accomplices rather than perpetrators. Similarly recognising patriarchy in society, Pollack suggested that women could benefit from the 'chivalry' of male criminal justice practitioners, and therefore recognised social structures as influential. As criminology evolved, and control theories, functionalism and anomie and labelling and interactions criminology became prominent, many criminologists tended to be stereotypically gender-blind.

> Remember that early criminology tended to make crude assumptions on the basis of biological myths. However it would be naïve to assume that such crude ideas have disappeared entirely!

The emergence of second wave feminism in the 1970s, and the publication of Freda Adler's *Sisters in Crime* (1975) did not herald the arrival of feminist criminology, instead, as Kathleen Daly has suggested, 'Feminist perspectives in criminology are a very recent development, having only begun to appear in criminal justice and criminology texts in the early 1990s (Daly, 1994: 121). That stated, while feminist perspectives are a somewhat recent arrival, the influence has been substantial and challenged the ideas of more traditional criminology (see table overleaf).

Masculinities and crime

Crime is something that is male-dominated, whether involving property or violence, the powerless or the powerful, from petty property crime to multi-million pound fraud, crime is something that is predominantly done by men. In the 1990s, criminology turned its attention to a new question, 'Why is crime predominantly a male activity?'

For feminists the answer was often found in the concept of patriarchy and all men having power over all women. Some male criminologists criticised this essentialism and the idea that all men could be placed in a universal category. They argued that men's experiences were different, and that men were divided and different in terms of the way that they enacted their masculine role. Therefore some social theorist's introduced the concept of 'hegemonic masculinity', which is a notion suggesting that at any given time, a commonly accepted and dominant form of 'being male' that is dominant in society in gender terms, subordinates other forms of masculinity and femininity. This dominant or 'hegemonic' form of masculinity will be visible in ideas, values, images and customs in that society at that time.

Traditional criminology:	Feminist criminology:
• was driven by biological assumptions created by male bias – men were superior, and there is a normal masculine and feminine type that can be linked with moral ideas	• highlighted inequality and the double standards of morality – for example, the way in which women are sexualised but men are not
• regarded female criminality as caused by biological factors and sexuality – for example, hormonal activities	• was keen to explore women's experiences in order to generate theories, particularly with regard oppression, patriarchy and inequality
• linked women's offending to biological causes; criminal women were mad, bad, passive, and deceitful, or a combination of these factors	• challenged the bias of traditional explanations of female criminality; highlighted the lack of appropriate attention given to women by criminologists
• showed scant regard for women's experience as victims, only as offenders	• raised the prominence of women's status as victims of abuse, both physical and economic
• was largely male-dominated and did not consider the male dominance in criminology or the criminal justice system worthy of investigation.	• emphasised the different social opportunities afforded to women because of male-dominated institutions and culture.

Crime as 'doing masculinity'

Much of the work on masculinity and crime has been authored by men, but it should be noted that many of these men have aligned themselves with feminist criminology, declaring themselves pro-feminist. In general terms masculinity is a concept perhaps most prominently associated with sociologist Robert Connell (1987, 1995), who initially challenged the feminist notion of 'patriarchy', suggesting that such assertions failed to display an understanding of the multiplicity of maleness.

James Messerschmidt made Connell's work directly relevant to crime. Messerschmidt challenged the essentialism of some feminist writers – that is, the notion, for example, that 'all men are violent and all women victims'. Messerschmidt argued that the divide between gender is best understood by drawing upon three factors; the gender division of Labour, and the gender relations of power and sexuality. Messerschmidt argued that only by looking at these three elements, at one particular time, could we begin to understand how gender identities are created.

Messerschmidt noted that 'men use the resources at their disposal to communicate their experiences to others' in other words, masculinity doesn't just exist, it has to be shown. It is in this show that 'for many men, crime serves as a "resource" for doing gender' (1993: 84). In other words, crime is one way that a man can show that he is a man.

"Why is crime predominantly the preserve of men?"

In answering this question you should be drawing upon the theories outlined in this chapter. Remember you can draw upon the notion of hegemonic masculinity proposed by Connell and furthered by Messerschmidt, but you could also draw upon some of the work of feminists. Also remember that biological explanations are relevant to these discussions and you might want to revisit that subject – Do differences in biology explain differences in law breaking? Background facts such as the ratio of male to female prison population are useful to weave into your answer.

Taking it **FURTHER**

Messerschmidt's *Masculinities and Crime* (1993) is still available, and students would find it useful in that it not only offers coverage of the issue of male crime, but provides an extremely worthy overview of 'traditional' criminology and feminist perspectives. You might want to think about what it might be that makes some crimes, such as football hooliganism, almost a uniquely male phenomena? An interesting account of the links between crime and criminality is Newburn and Stanko's (1995) *Just Boys Doing Business* which I would direct students toward.

Textbook guide

Most criminology textbooks will have a chapter on 'gender and crime' or 'women and crime', but can tend to neglect masculinity and crime as a subject area. In terms of feminist criminology, Daly and Maher's (1998) *Criminology at the Crossroads: feminist readings on crime and justice* contains writings by some of the most influential feminist criminologists. Sandra Walklate's (2004) *Gender, Crime and Criminal Justice* is a comprehensive textbook (now in its second edition) that gives the subject of gender and crime comprehensive coverage.

2.10

penology

Core areas: **What is penology?**

Why punish?

A brief history of British prison: Prison timeline

Historical phases of punishment

Are prisons in crisis?

The future of prisons

Running themes

Imprisonment and its effects and use should never be removed from **ideological** considerations, and therefore the stance that people take upon imprisonment will be influenced by their opinions and their beliefs in the purpose of punishment. Of course, there will also always be **political** and **economic** considerations that also inform how imprisonment is used. Clearly imprisonment and removing an individual's liberty is about the exercise of **power** by the state. Imprisonment should be considered in light of what we know about **gender**, **class** and **race** as there is a common theme of **inequality** when these factors are linked to imprisonment.

Key thinker

Michel Foucault (1926–84) was a French sociologist interested in the relationship between power and knowledge (a theme that is evident in the majority of his work). The power/knowledge complex is based on the idea that power and knowledge are intimately connected, and each is reliant upon the other. With regard the prison; Foucault suggests that power is not intrinsic in the institution, but in the techniques of discipline on which the prison draws. Foucault traces the development of institutions that draw upon discipline, such as the system of prisons, suggesting that there has been a visible spread in social control – and the growth of disciplinary society as a whole. *Discipline and Punish* (1977) documented the shift from corporal to carceral punishment between the late eighteenth and mid-nineteenth century.

What is penology?

Traditionally the term penology has been used to detail the academic study of penal institutions (in the most part, prisons). Penology, like criminology, has drawn from a diverse range of academic traditions; from psychology, medicine and economics through to social sciences. Traditionally the term penology was in the most part associated with attempts to reform and rationalise penal conditions (such as in the work of John Howard and Jeremy Bentham), but more recently, penology's focus broadened. Penology can now be seen to include the systematic inquiry into the characteristics of the penal institution (for example, the work of Goffman, 1961) and inquiry into the effectiveness of custody (this includes some work on the subject of legal theories and theories of punishment).

Why punish?

Theories about the purpose of punishment will necessarily underpin a large amount of penology. Those academics who write about and study imprisonment often have different and conflicting views about what prison should be for – what an individual regards as the purpose of imprisonment will clearly have an impact upon whether they regard punishment as effective or not. There are a number of competing views of the purposes of punishment, and you should be aware of these. Practically, prison is used to hold people on remand, (those who are awaiting trial but have been refused bail for fear that they will flee, interfere with the process of the law or commit further crimes), as a threat to support non-custodial sentences and as a punishment in its own right. Beyond the practical purposes there are a number of ideological justifications for imprisonment that have been used by a range of academics to support their arguments about imprisonment.

The symbolic function (denunciation) – By removing offenders from society and placing restrictions upon their liberty and freedoms, prison fulfils a symbolic function – it sends out a powerful message to both offenders and non-offenders that criminal behaviour is not tolerated and will evoke sanction. Prisons express the collective disapproval of the public for the actions of the offender. Often, Victorian local prisons are large buildings toward the centre of cities. Their architecture and positioning are perhaps good reminders of how the symbolic function of prison was actively conveyed to citizens.

Incapacitation – This is the idea that punishment generally (and prison specifically) actively serve to prevent people committing more crime. The offender's liberty is curtailed so that the individual is rendered physically incapable of further offending. Clearly while someone is in prison it is difficult for them to commit offences against the community at large for the length of their incarceration, but the notion of incapacitation informs a range of punishments. For example, in the 1960s, attendance centres were developed to prevent football hooligans from attending matches, and driving bans and electronic tagging can also serve as a means of incapacitating offenders.

Deterrence – This describes the notion that the threat of some form of consequence can serve to dissuade people from a course of action, and encourage them to abide by society's rules. The principle of deterrence was the basis of Beccaria's classical criminological work (1764), but has also been influential with politicians and academics, often (though not exclusively) those on the political right.

Rehabilitation – The concept of rehabilitation is often linked with treatment, and describes a concern with reforming or rehabilitating offenders, whether by personal example, or through training, education, work experience, or exposing offenders to treatment programmes, group work, and counselling. Such an approach views the sentence of imprisonment and the associated loss of liberty as the punishment, and argues for positive prison regimes that are humane and progressive in the belief that they can reduce the future occurrence of crime.

Retributivism – Essentially retributive suggests that the reason for punishing offenders is because they deserve it. The future consequences of the punishment are not an issue that needs to be considered; quite simply when the offender committed the offence they 'earned' the punishment.

Abolitionism – There is another important strand of thought on imprisonment that influences penology, 'abolitionism'. Abolitionism isn't really a theory about the purpose of punishment but about its delivery. If prison damages people and does them more harm than good (because of factors such as its negative effects upon employment prospects, its tendency to institutionalise, brutalise and sever family ties), should we use it at all? Abolitionists argue that because of the damage done by prison, we should remove or restrict its use. In the most extreme form, abolitionists call for the wholesale removal of prison sanctions, but most current abolitionists argue for prison to be a last resort and only used when necessary with the most serious and dangerous offenders.

A brief history of British prison

There is not really time to detail the whole history of the development of the British prison system, but many of criminology's core works are related to the development of punishment and forms of social control (see Foucault, 1977 and Garland, 2002). It is worth you having a knowledge not only of the theory with which we explain punishment and imprisonment, but also of some of the most important historical events in terms of British prisons and this list should help you somewhat toward that end.

Prison timeline

1777 – John Howard, religious reformer and former High sheriff of Bedfordshire publishes *The State of the Prison in England and Wales* and describes the system of local prisons as 'filthy, corrupt ridden and unhealthy'.

1779 – 'Hard labour' is introduced by parliament and prisoners are held on prison hulks (old ships) anchored in the river Thames. The use of these hulks is only discontinued in 1857.

1810 – The Holford Committee is established by parliament as a forum to debate imprisonment. They make the decision to build the first state penitentiary (Millbank) that will reform offenders through solitary confinement and rigorous religious instruction.

1816 – The first state-built prison, Millbank, opens in Central London.

1823 – Under Home Secretary Robert Peel, the Goal act is passed. This attempt to separate prisoners according to the crimes they had committed, proved largely ineffectual in practice.

1835 – The Prisons Act makes provisions for the appointment of five inspectors of prisons, while the dominant ideology remains isolating prisoners so that they cannot be a bad influence upon one another, a continuation of the ideas which informed the Goal act in 1823.

1862–68 – Both public flogging (in 1862) and Transportation (in 1868) are abolished as punishments.

1887 – The Prison Act 1887 first brought prisons under the control of the Home Secretary in Britain. Prior to this, prisons were administered locally by

(Continued)

(Continued)

justices of the peace. Administration of the Prison system is made the responsibility of a prison commission, and the first head of the commission Sir Edmund Du Cane is appointed. He is unflinching in his belief that prison should punish, and installs a harsh regime for prisoners.

1895 – The Gladstone Committee is progressive and suggests that a core function of prison should be to 'reform'. The recommendations are embraced by new head of the prison commission Sir Evelyn Ruggles Bryce. Prison conditions and regimes begin to improve in a period of 'penal welfarism' (see 'Phase 2' on page 104)

1895–1960s – An era of progressive penal policy and practice in Britain. 'Penal welfarism' is best characterised by Phase 2 (see page 104).

1960s – The first crisis of security and the Mountbatten report – a number of high profile escapes by Great Train Robbers, and Spy George Blake leads to an increased focus upon security – with resources increasingly targeted at preventing escape.

1974 – Robert Martinson publishes his 'What Works?' article which questions the effectiveness of treatment. With the political right gaining influence there is a decline in the influence of 'treatment' and welfare approaches and an increased belief that prison is effective as a means of incapacitation.

1990 – The Strangeways Riot – the largest prison disturbance in Britain – sparks a wave of riots and protests in other institutions, and highlights how stark and bleak conditions have become in prison, where an emphasis on security and overcrowded local prisons is brought to light.

1991 – Lord Woolfe's report into the Strangeways riot is published. It is extremely critical of the management and regime in prisons, and the lack of humanity and justice shown to prisoners, especially those on remand. The Criminal Justice Act makes provision for the contracting out of court escort services.

1992 – The Criminal Justice Act is extended to allow for new private prisons to be built to hold convicted prisoners.

1993 – Michael Howard makes his now famous 'Prison works' speech to the conservative party conference, which is inspired by American right realist Charles Murray. This is also the year that two-year-old James Bulger is murdered by two ten-year-old boys; an event that many criminologists regard as a catalyst for steep increases in the use of prison. Similarly, legislation allows all state prisons to be privately managed; with a target that 10% of prisons will be privately managed.

1994 – Woodcock report into the escape of armed prisoners from the special security unit at Whitemoor prison is extremely critical of lax security at the prison.

1995 – Three life sentence prisoners escape from Parkhurst Prison. The Learmont report is once again highly critical of security; Michael Howard sacks the Director General of the Prison Service, Derek Lewis. The legacy of the Parkhurst and Whitemoor escapes is increased security.

1997 – New Labour elected to power having promised to reverse prison privatisation, however once elected they continue its use.

1998 – Wormwood Scrubs prison is subjected to a police investigation that eventually sees three officers jailed for violence against prisoners and six officers dismissed (including three who had been convicted and cleared on appeal). Eventually The Prison Service admit that its officers subjected some inmates to sustained beatings, mock executions, death threats, choking and torrents of racist abuse.

2000 – Zahid Mubarek is attacked by his racist cellmate in his cell at Feltham Young Offenders institution. He died seven days later. The government's repeated attempts to block a public inquiry, led to a four-and-a-half year delay between the murder and the inquiry.

2003 – A review under the leadership of businessman Patrick Carter recommends the merger of the prison and probation service into the National Offender Management Service (NOM). The government accept this recommendation and work begins toward a merger.

2005 – The prison population in England and Wales reaches 76,226 on the first of July, its highest ever, it is predicted to rise to above 80,000 shortly, and be 90,000 by the end of the decade.

Historical phases of punishment

Prison and punishment are evolutionary, and many academics have documented change in the administration of punishment. Michel Foucault's (1977) suggestion that the development of prison can be linked to the emergence of a disciplinary industrial society has been built upon by academics, such as David Garland (2001a), who broadly divide punishment into three phases:

Phase 1

The first phase was marked by the use of capital and corporal punishment, prior to the increasing reliance upon prison. This is a time where capital punishment was commonplace largely prior to the birth of industrial society. Humanitarians and religious reformers such as those of the 'classical school' challenge the harsh and erratic nature of punishment.

Phase 2

The second phase witnesses society's industrialisation, and with it the spread of a discipline society. Capital and corporal punishments are reduced and instead 'carceral' punishment takes its place: prison, reformatories and poor houses. The ideology that underpins such notions is more welfare-orientated and new disciplines such as psychiatry and psychology offer the potential solutions for treating and reforming offenders, and instilling discipline spreads.

Phase 3

The third phase occurs post-1960s and is set against a backdrop of increased political discussion about crime and punishment. This phase also witnesses the decline in welfarism, the belief that 'nothing works' and a growing public 'punitivism'. Notions of treatment decline, to be replaced by the concept of 'risk management'. Levels of incarceration rise and we witness the birth of mass incarceration. The spread of technology means that custody extends beyond the prison wall and into society more generally (for example, satellite monitoring, or electronic tagging).

Are prisons in crisis?

The notion of the British prison system being in crisis is not new, but rather part of a continuing trend. Prison escapes, prison riots, suicides, an increasing prison population and unrest between staff and inmates are part of a long running trend; and media and academic accounts have been common currency for some 20 years (Cavidino and Dignan, 2002: 9).

The contested nature of the prison crisis

For some academics, particularly those on the political left, and those who subscribe in some way to abolitionist philosophy, the crisis in our prisons is evident in a number of ways: the overcrowding in prison; the violence; the incidents of self-harm and suicide; the levels of prisoners with mental illness; and drug addiction and health problems, all serve as examples of the crisis. However other academics, particularly those on the political right such as right realists, see no real crisis because they believe in prison effectiveness as a means of incapacitation, and therefore do not necessarily believe that prisons are in crisis.

The problem with the term crisis is that it tends to suggest something that is short lived, ever worsening and likely to have notable consequences. While there are express concerns with the state of prisons, on a day-to-day basis, 'crisis' is perhaps not the best term that we could use to describe the conditions in prison, the term does convey the sense that there is a need for action. We have, as Cavidino and Dignan note, 'reached a critical juncture' (2002: 11), and with increasing numbers projected in the prison population, we need to think carefully and consider the state and function of our prisons. There are four accounts of the prison crisis (see below).

Prison Crisis

Orthodox accounts of the 'crisis' in prisons see the crisis as the result of a number of interconnected factors: high prison numbers; overcrowding; conditions in prison; understaffing and staff unrest; poor security; the toxic mix of lifers and mental ill prisoners; and a breakdown of control.

Radical accounts of the penal crisis were also previously used by Cavidino and Dignan (in 1997) only to be omitted from the later edition of their book (2002). The radical account, they argue, is associated with the work of Mike Fitzgerald and Joe Sim. They suggest there are five components of the prison crisis in prisons:

1 **Conditions**
Bad conditions in prison

2 **Containment**
Security, riots, overcrowding

3 **Visibility**
Concerning the secrecy of prisons

4 **Authority**
Prison officers' experiences as their role is challenged and changed

5 **Legitimacy**
Power which is morally justified or fair.

Critical mainstream, referred to in the second edition of Cavidino and Dignan's (2002) book *The Penal System*, was principally an account of the crisis given by Anthony Bottoms. Bottoms (1980) suggested that the crisis was in part due to the collapse of a rehabilitative ideal that accompanied the work of Martinson, and in part due to limited resources available within prisons. Bottoms recognised that the crisis in imprisonment was both ideological and economic, however, the growth of the 'what works?' movement from the 1980s and the government's limited re-commitment to rehabilitation may have served to limit the usefulness of this theory in terms of contemporary debate.

Radical pluralist sees the orthodox account as unduly positivistic, and suggests that the crisis in prisons is the result of varying, potentially interconnected elements drawn from the above accounts. These will interact in a highly complex manner which contains both material and ideological elements. This most complex account of the prison crisis acknowledges the widest range of components and presents the most comprehensive picture. The radical pluralist account suggests that the crisis in imprisonment is the result of a crisis of legitimacy; but also acknowledges that prisons have to be legitimate to three groups:

1 Public

2 Staff

3 Prisoners

If prisons fail to act legitimately to any of these groups, symptoms of the crisis will occur; riots, political problems, industrial relations problems or public outrage.

The future of prisons

In both America and Britain from the late 1970s there has been a largely unbroken trend of increased prison numbers. This has accompanied what I have termed the move toward Phase 3 in imprisonment, the shift from rehabilitative to post-welfare mass imprisonment (Parenti, 1999; Garland, 2001b). As the crisis in prison numbers grows ever greater in the capitalist west, it is likely that prisons and imprisonment, their legitimacy and the existence of a 'crisis', will be the subject of fierce academic debate for years to come.

❝ To what extent can the prison service be said to be in crisis? ❞

Remember that you have at your disposal four models that have been used to explain the prison crisis and these could be used in the context of your argument. Questions such as this will almost always allow you to show knowledge of contemporary developments, and it is worth having some facts at your disposal. Try to be contemporary, so if talking about prison numbers you would be well advised to know how many people are currently imprisoned in Britain (many students quite simply get such details wrong). Remember that the contested purpose of punishment and the multiple stakeholders within prisons make the very function of imprisonment contested; with some unwilling to accept that there is a crisis (such as right realist Charles Murray) through to those who favour abolitionism. Try to represent all sides of the argument but don't be afraid to come to your own conclusion based upon the evidence you have.

Taking it **FURTHER**

The timeline on pages 101–103 lists some key historical developments in British prisons. Having knowledge of these will undoubtedly be of use to you and there are a number of good books on imprisonment written by academics that will detail these developments in more detail. You might find it useful to read up on these, and I would recommend Cavidino and Dignan's (2002) *The Penal System* for this purpose.

The critical mainstream account suggests that the crisis in rehabilitation was responsible for the crisis in imprisonment, and this in part was inspired by the work of Robert Martinson, who was a liberal academic best remembered for his study of the effectiveness of rehabilitative schemes. Read Martinson's work (1974) in order to critically evaluate the proposition that any decline in rehabilitative approaches is driven by political motivation and the growing politics of law and order. Perhaps you might try reading Martinson's arguments and seeing whether you agree with how they have been represented.

Textbook guide

Michael Cavidino and James Dignan's (2002) *The Penal System* is now in its third edition and is an extremely comprehensive and authoritative account of the issues surrounding imprisonment. Joe Sim's chapter (2004) 'Thinking about Imprisonment' in Muncie and Wilson's *Student Handbook of Criminal Justice and Criminology* offers an excellent concise contemporary insight into the ideology and political thinking behind imprisonment. Students should also try reading a prisoner's account of their experiences, and there is none better that Edwin James' (2003) *A Life Inside*.

2.11

serious crime

Core areas: **White collar crime**

Organisational and corporate crimes

Professional crime

Organised crime

Trans-national crime

War crimes and genocide

Running themes

I have used the term 'serious crime' to describe a range of criminal activity. For criminologists examining white collar crimes, issues of **power** and **representation** are combined. They suggest (in the critical/conflict tradition) that the crimes of the powerful are given very little attention and that most criminology is driven by a perception where the crimes committed by the relatively powerless are prioritised. This form of criminology seeks to challenge and re-consider what constitutes criminal acts, arguing that a wider appreciation of criminal activity is necessary; and criminologists should broaden their focus to examine crimes of the state and crimes of the elite.

Key thinker

Edwin H. Sutherland (1883–1950). The concept of white collar crime (WCC) stems from the work of American Sociologist Edwin H. Sutherland. Sutherland specifically sought an opportunity to prove that his theory of differential association (see Chapter 2.3) could account for all forms of criminality. Sutherland defined WCC as 'A crime committed by a person of responsibility in the course of his [*sic*] occupation' (Sutherland 1945; 1949) a definition that has now been heavily criticised (see below). However it should be noted that by shifting the attention away from the emphasis on poverty and other problems located amongst the lower socio-economic classes (that was so dominant in the criminology of the time), Sutherland had set the scene for conflict theories and promoted the idea that crime was something that spanned all classes.

What images does the word crime evoke in your mind? Most of us if we were to be honest would immediately think about crime being serious; and would probably think of crimes such as murder, robbery, theft and burglary. We associate crime with inner-city areas, with poverty and harshness of life. It is not surprising therefore that when criminologists examine crime, when politicians and the public discuss it and the media report it, it is just these sorts of 'crimes of the street' that are represented. Few of us associate crime with wealthy businessmen in expensive suits, yet nevertheless, that is perhaps where crime is at its most prevalent and has the greatest cost to society. This chapter examines serious crime, which is largely crime involving more powerful and privileged actors.

White collar crime

Sociologist Edwin Sutherland argued that the rich and powerful commit crimes, and that included 'white collar workers' (who are a higher occupational class than their blue collar counterparts). White collar offenders were executive and business manager level. Sutherland argued that those of a higher status, and enjoying a higher degree of trust were also frequently likely to be the perpetrators of a range of crimes and misdemeanours, but were less likely to be detected and prosecuted. As you will already be aware, Sutherland was keen for criminology to extend its focus beyond the notion of crime, and examine socially harmful activity (see Chapter 1.5).

White collar crime is regarded by most criminologists as potentially far more harmful and serious than other types of crime, however, it is infrequently acknowledged in such a way by society generally, and may tend to be little conceived or understood by many members of society.

'White collar crime' as a category has been used to refer to an extremely diverse and varied collection of criminal activities, from smaller frauds committed by junior office staff in small businesses, to multi-million pound frauds committed by the directors of multi-national corporations. Therefore what constitutes white collar crime is not really agreed upon. Instead the term tends to be deployed in a varying fashion. However in the most part the term still describes any:

- offences committed by people of high/or relatively high status
- offences committed in the workplace by people who enjoy fairly privileged positions of trust
- offences that one made possible by legitimate employment
- typical offences considered under this category, including: accounting malpractice, frauds, embezzlement, tax evasion/violation and workplace related thefts.

There are immediate problems with the concept of white collar crime: What do we mean by high status? How should we define and measure it? How do we measure and categorise privilege? Although Sutherland makes it quite clear that he is detailing the higher echelons of organisational hierarchy, the term 'white collar crime' has often been used to categorise any crime that is not committed by manual (or blue collar) workers. The problem with this approach is that it tends to move away from the original concern with examining the illegitimate behaviour of the privileged. As the problems with identifying exactly what constitutes 'white collar crime' are many, some academics, such as Richard

Quinney (1977) have argued that the term 'white collar crime' should be replaced, and all crimes committed in the course of employment should be referenced under the heading 'occupational crime'.

Hazel Croall suggests that 'the enormous range of activities encompassed by the category of white collar crime has inevitably led to attempts to divide it into sub-categories, to provide researchers with a manageable group of offences and enable comparisons between offences' (Croall, 2001: 11). It is therefore important that criminologists do not consider 'white collar crime' a set of neat, easily-defined offences.

The most significant debate around white collar crime in recent years has been that involving the distinction between **occupational** *and* **organisational** *crime.*

- **Occupational crime** *is the category given by Quinney where people commit crime in the course of their employment, in the main for personal gain*
- **Organisational crime** *is essentially corporate crime, where the aim is to further the purposes of the company, but not necessarily the individual.*

What are not disputed by most criminologists are the serious potential implications of failures in individual and corporate practices. Carson's study of the loss of life in the exploration for oil in the North Sea (confirmed by later events such as the blowing up of the Alpha oil rig in 1988 with the loss of 168 lives), for instance, showed that many lives could have been saved with rudimentary attention to safety considerations (Carson, 1981). The chemical explosion at the Union Carbide Company in Bhopal (which killed 2,600 people) serves as an example of how great the cost can be when companies breach health and safety regulations. Similarly the Transport and general workers union have suggested that between April 2002 and March 2004, 620 workers were killed at the workplace in Britain; with as many as three in five deaths within the workplace due to health and safety breaches.

There are, however, some criminologists that have contested the idea that white collar crime should constitute an area of study for criminologists. For Gottfredson and Hirschi (1990), much white collar crime mirrors traditional crime, and can be explained using 'control theory' (offenders seek immediate gratification) which renders the setting of crime and status of the offender an irrelevance. Other criminologists have been quick to ridicule the notion of white collar crime; hence prominent right realist James Q. Wilson's dismissive suggestion that:

'People do not bar and nail shut their windows, avoid going out at night or harbor deep suspicions about strangers because of unsafe working conditions or massive consumer fraud' (1975).

Organisational and corporate crimes

Sutherland's work proved influential in that it lead criminologists to question the occurrence of crime as part of capitalism; influencing conflict criminology, much of which was Marxist inspired and critical of capitalism and its institutions. This in turn influenced criminologists to turn their attention to how crime and business could be linked and resulted in the study of organisational or corporate crime.

The term corporate crime is used to refer to both acts and omissions that are the result of deliberate decisions or negligence in legitimate businesses. These acts are undertaken not to benefit an individual or individuals, but by individuals in order to benefit the corporation itself, and therefore reflect upon the culture of the company. By breaking laws (both civil and criminal) it is possible for companies, for example, to chase greater profits at the cost of employee or public safety. Such an activity is not individually motivated but part of the ethos of the company. While it may sometimes be called 'organisational' crime it should not be confused with 'organised' crime.

Professional crime

Once again the term 'professional crime' can trace its origins to Edwin Sutherland and specifically his life history study of Chic Conwell (who actually wrote the majority of the text), *The Professional Thief* (1937). Sutherland suggests that being a professional thief required that one made a living by exclusively committing thefts, and using all of ones working hours illegitimately. The core intention of this work was to provide empirical support for the concepts that criminal activity is planned, and more importantly learned by 'differential association'.

The notion of criminal careers continued to gain influence in criminality, however, the term 'criminal career' has bypassed and replaced the notion of 'professional crime'. The problem with this is that they do not necessarily refer to the same thing. Those involved in crime will all have a criminal career, even if it is short; the notion of professional criminality conveys a sense of the persistent commitment that some, but by no means all offenders have to crime. However, professional crime is inherently difficult to define; as you have to ask on what grounds do we assess 'professionalism' in terms of crime, by competence or commitment? Who constitutes the professional criminal? However, the term has been used by criminologists examining some more serious and organised forms of criminality.

Organised crime

It is perhaps unsurprising that most of the discussion of organised crime emanates from America around the 1920s, an era where prohibition of alcohol created the climate for 'boot-leggers' to accumulate vast personal wealth through the illegal sale of alcohol. However, over time it has emerged as a concept to be used by both academics and political groups; emerging again as an area of interest in the post-communist era, until 2001 when both political groups and academics turned there attention to new criminal threats to national security from organised criminal gangs such as the Russian mafia. In recent years, and post-September 11th, this concern is being replaced with the threat of terrorism, somewhat displacing discussions about organised crime.

Indeed in the wake of the terrorist attacks on the London underground on 7 July 2004, the need to tackle organised crime has really been eclipsed by discussions about terrorism. Perhaps what is notable here is that, very often, the two can co-exist, and it has long been known that terrorist organisations often have links to highly organised forms of criminality. In the aftermath of the terrorist attacks in London, debate quickly turned to the failure of legislation allowing criminals to be tracked across national borders that mirror earlier debates about organised crime groups. However, there has been less attention paid to the way the political actions of some state governments have served to assist such groups previously, although there has been some discussion about how some state governments actively continue to support and cultivate terrorism.

The specific threat of organised crime is apparent in that criminal behaviour associated with professional crime threatens and relies upon institutions of power, for example, corrupting government figures, 'buying people off', and bid rigging, but similarly, as many of the activities of large criminal groups mirror the activities of the state, exacting money, threatening the state's core functions of protection, extraction and coercion along with the state's monopoly on force (Naylor, 1997).

Trans-national crime

The concept of trans-national crime relies a great deal on the sociological concept of globalisation, which is a term that sociologists use to describe the way the world is transformed into a single global system; and the way in which the world is shrinking with the introduction of new technology, the expansion of international trade and the international distribution of labour.

Globalisation and the changing nature of the world create new criminal opportunities – some via new technology such as computers and the internet, some because of the expansion of markets. Globalisation is an important element, as whilst trans-national crime has occurred for many years (think of smuggling as an example, which has occurred for centuries) the changing world we live in clearly presents new opportunities for criminals. What is meant by trans-national crime, is crime that involves a fairly high degree of sophistication and organisation, often the endeavour of criminal gangs who can use national borders to avoid law enforcement agencies.

Some key features of trans-national crime

- At the most basic level, trans-national crime is crime that crosses national boundaries, and therefore crosses different countries with different laws and law enforcement agencies
- It is regarded in the most part as sophisticated – the product of calculating criminal gangs
- It often involves illicit markets, such as the traffic in illegal drugs, firearms, products made from endangered species, people trafficking
- Some items, however, may be legal, such as smuggling of legal goods to avoid paying duty (such as tobacco, alcohol or antiques)
- It may well involve corruption and using legitimate companies as a front; corruption underlies a great deal of trans-national crime (bribing officials, moving and laundering money)
- Statutory controls such as immigration controls or high taxes create the markets that trans-national criminals rely upon
- Moral campaigners have highlighted the trade in human organs and children and babies sold for adoption, but again these issues are less frequently considered as trans-national crime.

War crimes and genocide

War crimes are acts that are criminal and remain criminal, even though they are committed by individuals or groups at a time of war or armed conflict when acting under military orders. Acts such as murder, torture, ill treatment or slave labour of civilians; the murder or torture of prisoners of war; killing hostages; the destroying of property civilian settlements unnecessarily, could all constitute war crimes. Members of armed forces, militias, or civilians who violate such laws can be tried by international and national courts and military tribunals. It is not a defence to cite acting under orders, however, superior officers hold a responsibility for those under their direction unless they have evidently attempted to suppress them. The 1949 Geneva Convention clarified the war crimes accepted by the Nuremburg Trial of leading Nazis, and subsequent rules have extended the protections available to soldiers and civilians at times of conflict. However, this has not prevented such crimes, which not only include such crimes as the massacre of civilians in Srebrenica and Rwanda, but also occur in the now occupied Iraq, and are the preserve of both British and American soldiers. Some criminologists have highlighted failure of criminology to adequately examine war crime.

Genocide refers to organised acts of crime that are committed during either conflict or peace, and intend to exterminate all or part of a national, religious, racial or ethnic group. It differs from what is termed 'ethnic cleansing' because it is state-sponsored and organised, as in the case of the treatment of the Jews by Nazi Germany. Genocide is regarded by the United Nation's general assembly to be the most serious crime against humanity, however, once again, criminologists have been slow to regard this as a viable field of inquiry. Genocide, like war crime and all of the crimes above, is largely committed by those who are privileged, yet any searching of criminology textbooks will quickly reveal the fact that it is a crime that criminologists have ignored. This perhaps serves as further evidence of criminologist failure to engage with the crimes of the powerful and elite due to their pre-occupation with crimes of the street.

❝ Has criminology as a subject adequately recognised or addressed the crimes of the powerful? ❞

This question or similar questions about the focus of criminology are often seen as a gift by students in exams because they allow you to expand a debate to a wide range of areas. However, you should beware of the 'all I know about' answer because, all too frequently, students rush into writing what ends up a very jumbled and mixed answer. Try to write to a structure; so you might want to say, 'there are a variety of areas that I could examine [give examples] but in this instance I will focus upon the crimes of the state specifically'. If you do this then make sure that you stay to the brief you set yourself. Remember to draw upon theory (in this case the work of conflict and left idealist criminologists lends empirical support). Remember to use and cite theorists, so you can mention specific contributions made by academics. If doing this in exams try to remember the date and title of publications, it shows you have done some revision.

Taking it **FURTHER**

Is James Q. Wilson right to argue that 'People do not bar and nail shut their windows, avoid going out at night or harbor deep suspicions about strangers because of unsafe working conditions or massive consumer fraud'? Are the crimes of the powerful really threatening or are they an essential part of life? One of the problems with the crimes of the powerful is that we simply have very little knowledge about the real extent (because of their hidden nature; a point Wilson fails to make). If you had to go about researching corporate or white collar crime, how would you go about it? What are the difficulties in finding out about victims? Would it ever be possible to overcome these?

Textbook guide

Gary Slapper and Steve Tomb's *Corporate Crime* (1999) book offers a comprehensive and accessible text for students, especially with regard to policing and punishment of corporate crime. Maurice Punches' (1996) *Dirty Business* is also a useful text on the subject of corporate crime. Stephen Box's (1983) *Power, Crime and Mystification* is an excellent account of the crimes of the powerful, as is Eugene McLaughlin's chapter in Muncie and McLaughlin's *The Problem of Crime* (2001) as it considers terrorism and political violence committed by the state. Most criminological textbooks will have a section on white collar crime.

2.12	
victimology	

Core areas: **Victimology**

Early victimology

Labelling, victims and 'victimless crime'

Feminist criminology, domestic violence
and victimisation

Left realism and victimology

Right realism and victims

Critical victimology

Victims and restorative justice

Running themes

Clearly the relationship between victim and offender is one of **power**, and victimology is concerned with this, but it is also concerned with the power relationship between the victim and the agencies of the state and the criminal justice system. The criminal justice system can further **discriminate** against victims of crime. Victimology is also concerned with **inequality**, and how factors such as **gender**, **class** and **race** can result in **inequality** in terms of the experience of victimisation and the state response. Victimology similarly is linked to the study of people's perception of the likelihood of becoming a victim and the fear of crime, and therefore is also concerned with **representations** of crime.

Key thinker

John Braithwaite, in *Crime, Shame and Reintegration* (1989), put forward the suggestion that the key to crime control is a cultural commitment to what he termed 'reintegrative shaming' of lawbreakers. He suggests that some societies have higher crime rates than others because of the different processes of shaming wrong-doers. He accepts that shaming can be counterproductive, and can serve to increase crime problems, but suggests that when shaming is done within a cultural context of respect for the offender, it can be an extraordinarily powerful and efficient form of social control. Braithwaite's work is often regarded as the theoretical origins of 'restorative justice'.

Victimology

Victimiology is the term that is used to detail the specific study of those who are the victims of crime. It was by the 1970s that the academics began to be specifically concerned with the experiences of the victims of crime, and less concerned with relationships between victim and offender. Victimology is now sometimes regarded as a sub-discipline of criminology. It has developed significantly from attempts to map the characteristics of victims (in a similar fashion to that of early criminology and its attempts to map and define types of criminals) to focus upon the social and structural factors that influence the incidents and experience of victimisation. Similarly the background of researchers in the field of victimology has become more diverse, and in recent years victimology has been drawn increasingly from feminist and critical criminology.

Early victimology

Early criminological studies on victims sought to examine whether some people were more likely to be victims of crimes than others. More specifically, some sought to establish whether some responsibility for the crime lay with the victim, perhaps as a result of the victim's susceptibility to victimisation; or the victim's participation in the events that led to the crime. Typically, these early positivistic research studies emphasised the ways that victims can contribute to their victimisation. These studies created a climate within which policy-makers could obviate some of the responsibility for crime causation through a process of victim-blaming, but said little of the role of the state and its agencies.

Positivist victimology

Early victimology is often referred to as 'positivist victimology' because of the epistemology that informs it, however, not all criminologists use this term. If you see the term positivist victimology it is likely that it is talking about early victimisation studies.

Some examples of early victimology

- Hans Von Hentig's *The Criminal and the Victim* (1948) provided an analysis of the relationships between murderers and their victims by categorising victims according to their behaviour and vulnerability. He argued that the victim was not as a passive sufferer but that the victimisation could be a result of the victim's own precipitation of, or proneness to, the crime.
- Wolfgang's *Patterns in Criminal Homicide* (1958) provided support for Von Hentig's argument. In a study of 588 murder cases in Philadelphia, Wolfgang concluded that in 26% of the murders, the victims had 'initiated' the events that led to their death.
- Amir's study *Patterns of Forcible Rape* (1971) (like many studies subsequent to Wolfgang and Von Hentig) sought to apply the concept of victim precipitation to an inter-personal crime, and served to further 'blame the victim' (Amir's was perhaps the most controversial of early victim studies – he adopted a broader and more imprecise concept of 'victim precipitation' in an analysis of the victim-offender relationship in rape cases; the attribution of responsibility and blame to the victim in such cases has been strongly condemned). It should also be remembered that at the time of publication of Amir's study, feminists were starting to challenge Amir's perspective which they regarded as perpetuating the insidious myth that women invite rape (for example, by wearing the 'wrong' type of clothes or by walking down the 'wrong' unlit street).

It should be remembered that victim participation is not just an abstract theoretical concept, it is also evident in the justice process. Sexist and racist assumptions serve to undermine crimes such as rape and domestic violence and do little to explain victimisation. For example, the murder of Stephen Lawrence highlighted how the police initially perceived Stephen (a young black male) to be in some way 'responsible' for his victimisation. Due to the impact of feminism and more radical criminology, such bias assumptions have been challenged. However, it would be naïve to assume that such myth-driven racist (and sexist) assumptions do not continue to exist and examples of 'victim-blaming' are not still an intrinsic part of the criminal justice system and wider society.

Labelling, victims and 'victimless crime'

The labelling of individuals as 'criminal' has attracted much debate and criticism but there has been little critical consideration of the meanings attached to or associated with the label 'victim'. It is often a pejorative, value-laden and problematic designation. Elsewhere feminists have rejected the label 'victim' as they regard it as stigmatising and dis-empowering, preferring the term 'survivor' for those who have lived through sexual and physical abuse.

> You should avoid seeing 'criminals' and 'victims' as polar opposites, since we know that a great many criminals will have also experienced victimisation.

In 1965 Edwin Schur wrote *Crimes Without Victims*, in which he discussed problems associated with the creation and enforcement of particular crimes including homosexuality, drug use and addiction, and abortion. He suggested that such offences were victimless, and simply involved the 'willing exchange, amongst adults, of strongly demanded but legally prohibited goods and services' (1965: 169). Schur suggested that laws which prohibited such types of behaviour created disrespect for the law. Similarly when people fell into groups that were involved in such activities, they begin to form deviant identities. This identity could become so significant that it would eventually serve to prevent some individuals returning to the conventional world, even if they so desired.

The concept of *Crimes Without Victims* has now been widely challenged and has no real credibility, quite simply because crimes without victims do not exist. If we take drug addicts, for example, the victim may create costs for the state in terms of treatment, or may be unable to engage in a legitimate occupation due to their addiction. Others would suggest that the addict, or their family, can be construed as the victim, and more still would point to the way in which the drug trade is based upon violence and victimisation in a broader sense.

Feminist criminology, domestic violence and victimisation

During the 1970s the women's movement began to draw attention to the suffering of women in the private sphere (largely in the home). However, Hill and Wright (2004) have highlighted how at that time the problem was understood largely in terms of the victims' own inadequate personalities. This was often because it was the male professionals who were explaining domestic violence. Many criminal justice professionals asked why women in violent relationships did not leave their violent partners? They implied that it was not only irrational for women to stay, but that because they did, they were responsible for their own continued victimisation. Feminist researchers, on the other hand, began to point to the very rational reasons why women stayed in violent relationships. They did this by shifting from a positivist approach to an interpretivist approach where they engaged more with those who had experienced victimisation and generated knowledge about what it is like to be an abused woman, much of which confounded rather than confirmed traditional views.

Left realism and victimology

The break with left idealism that resulted in left realism was, as you have already seen (in Chapter 2.5) largely due to the concern that left idealism did not take crime or the experiences of victimisation as seriously as it should. Therefore, early left realist crime surveys underscored the way in which those who were socially excluded suffered more greatly the ill effects of crime (the poor, ethnic minorities and women suffered the most).

The left realist approach fixes the victim in the equation of the 'square of crime' (see page 59), a model which explains the crime rate as a consequence of the interaction between the agencies of social control, such as the state, the offender, the public and the victim. In this way, left realists tried to avoid the positivist tendency to indulge in victim-blaming (see Chapter 2.5).

The concept of the 'square of crime' minimises any division between victim and offender and maximises the sense that crime involves a relationship. For left realists, the impact of crime and victimisation depends upon, among other things, the response by state agencies such as the police and the courts. A consequence of inappropriate or unsympathetic responses from such agencies, for instance, if a victim-blaming response is evident, the result is further stigmatisation of the victim, often referred to as 'secondary victimisation'. This is an important concept as it highlights the way in which it is not only the criminal act that does harm – the response to the criminal act from state agencies can also be harmful to the victim.

Secondary victimisation is a concept that stems from left realist criminology. It describes how victims can be victimised by the primary criminal offence, and then re-victimised by the acts or omissions of the criminal justice system.

Right realism and victims

Although right realists have little to say about the experience of victimisation, their political philosophy is one of deterrence and punishment. Therefore without any real focus upon the experience of victimisation they have promoted more punitive, deterrent interventions. More recently some criminologists have questioned the role that victimology can play in proving the justification required by the political right to introduce harsher sentences for perpetrators. An example is how Michael Howard's 'Prison works' speech in 1993 was followed shortly afterwards by promises to 'put victims at the centre of the criminal justice process'. These approaches often boil down to a simplistic equation where increased rights for the victim equal greater losses for the offender.

Critical victimology

Critical victimology essentially takes its lead from critical criminology, with which it shares common features, but emphasises that victimisation is associated with structural powerlessness. This view of victimisation recognises that the impact of criminal victimisation is made more complex by factors such as age, sex and race. Critical victimology due to its reliance upon notions such as 'patriarchy' shared a concern with highlighting the hidden and complex nature of some forms of victimisation (for example, the abuse of children and the elderly). As a concept it is associated with Ron Mawby and Sandra Walklate's (1994) *Critical Victimology*. A critical approach to the issue of victimisation looks to the structure of society in which those crimes take place and asks uncomfortable questions about the adequacy of the response by the state for some victims. The low levels of policing and prosecution relating to some types of crime (such as corporate crime and crime that occurs in the private sphere) suggest that the criminal justice system itself is complicit in further victimising individuals. This is an important point since it challenges the ideological view that 'get tough' approaches can be justified on the grounds that it demonstrates the willingness of the state to take the needs of victims seriously.

Victims and restorative justice

Restorative justice is a concept that has only really gained momentum in recent years, but has had a quite profound impact upon criminology and more specifically victimology.

In *Crime, Shame and Reintegration* (1989) John Braithwaite attempted to outline an alternative strategy that promoted a radically different criminal justice policy, based upon models where re-integrative shaming forms the model for punishing transgressions of society's rules. Framing his work particularly around the justice of Aborigines in Australia, he argued that low crime societies were those that successfully balanced shame for the offender's actions with a concern for the individual support and validation for that person. Braithwaite has proved influential in academic argument and contributed to a growing momentum for criminal justice practice based upon 'restorative justice' principles.

There are a wide range of definitions of what 'restorative justice' involves, but regardless of the specifics of definition, it tends to equate with making amends, paying back, forgiveness and moving forward, making restorative justice in the most part a 'peacemaking' approach. One of the most commonly accepted definitions in Britain suggests that 'Restorative Justice is a process whereby parties with a stake in a specific offence collectively resolve how to deal with the aftermath of the offence and its implication for the future' (Marshall, 1999).

In the 1990s, 'restorative justice' became a principle to a wide range of ideas and practices in criminal justice systems, and those schemes that unite victim, offender and community, which exist across a range of societies. That stated, as definitions tend to vary, a bewildering and diverse range of programmes and schemes have been placed under the banner of 'restorative justice'. This is in part because restorative justice owes much of its appeal to the fact that it promotes inclusive roles for those often neglected in the criminal justice process, bringing both victims and offenders to the centre stage. Therefore the development of restorative justice should be considered part of a wider strategy to include victims in the criminal justice process.

While restorative justice has had a number of fierce advocates, in one of the few texts to examine the more negative aspects of a restorative approach, Declan Roche suggested that 'for all its promise of promoting healing and harmony, restorative justice can deliver a justice as cruel and vengeful as any' (2003: 1). Part of the problem is that due to differences in definition, and ideological disagreements regarding concepts such as shame, there exist fundamental differences in individuals views about what restoration should involve. Should offenders be *made* to feel 'guilt' for their acts, or *forced* to say sorry?

Common pitfall: There are some fierce advocates of restorative approaches, but there are fewer accounts that really criticise restorative justice. Try not to fall into the trap of regarding restorative justice as a 'solution' to the problem of crime.

You might want to try answering this question as if it were a 45 minute written exam question.

"A restorative justice scheme calls a conference which was convened for a 12-year-old boy caught shoplifting. The proposal of his mother that he should stand outside the shop wearing a T-shirt emblazoned with the words 'I am a thief' all day on a Saturday was agreed with the store manager – Do you think this is a good idea? How can you support your answer with criminological theory? "

You can address this question using an 'advantages and disadvantages' approach (see Part 3). Use the information in this section on restorative justice as a guide, however, you should not forget that labelling/interactionist theory could also be used here. What might be the negative aspects of such an intervention? Is Schur right to argue that it might be better to do nothing? How is the young person going to experience re-intergration rather than simply shame alone?

Taking it **FURTHER**

Although the concept of victim-precipitation was supposedly designed to provide a value-neutral explanation of victimisation, we have seen that such neutrality does not exist and that we need to question the values upon which some judgements are made. As you will now be aware, it has often been women who have been held responsible for inviting victimisation, whereas men have not. Whether someone is constructed as 'blameless' or 'culpable', and is viewed as either a 'worthy' or 'unworthy' 'victim', often depends upon sexist, racist or class-based assumptions (see Hill and Wright, 2004)

Textbook guide

Victimology and more specifically restorative justice are two of the growth subjects in criminology at present, and new publications seem to be appearing at quite a rate. In terms of readings on the subject of victimisation and victims, Ron Mawby and Sandra Walklate's *Critical Victimology* (1994) was long considered the authoritative text on victims by many criminologists. In it, Mawby and Walklate sought to promote an understanding of victim issues in the criminal justice system. It is still a useful book, but is now somewhat dated and is perhaps a little complex as an introduction. I would suggest that Hill and Wright's (2004) chapter in John Muncie and David Wilson's *Student Handbook of Criminology and Criminal Justice* is the best concise introduction to victimology.

part three*
study writing and revision skills

Chapters: 3.1 **General introduction**

3.2 **Dealing with theory**

3.3 **How to get the most out of your lectures**

3.4 **How to get the most out of your seminars**

3.5 **Essay writing tips**

3.6 **Revision hints and tips**

3.7 **Exam tips**

*in collaboration with David McIlroy

3.1

general introduction

Success in any course will not simply come about by developing knowledge of theory; instead you will need to be able to demonstrate that you have a comprehensive grasp of the subject matter, and that you can apply theory. To this end, university degrees and criminology courses are likely to require some form of assessment. It is true to suggest that ultimately the knowledge that you gain as part of a degree course is only one part of the learning experience. If you are successful on a university degree you will acquire an array of transferable skills that will assist you in gaining employment. Therefore, this book intends to combine theoretical knowledge of criminology with useful practical guidance about how to undertake study. If you work your way through this chapter you should, at the end, be better equipped to profit from your lectures, benefit from your seminars, construct your essays efficiently, develop effective revision strategies and respond comprehensively to the pressures of exam situations.

In the six sections that lie ahead you will be presented with:

- Checklists and bullet points to focus your attention on key issues
- Exercises to help you participate actively in the learning experience
- Illustrations and analogies to enable you to anchor learning principles in everyday events and experiences
- Worked examples to demonstrate the use of such features as structure, headings and continuity
- Tips that provide practical advice that will benefit you in your study of criminology.

In the exercises that are presented you should decide how much effort you would like to invest in each exercise, according to your individual preferences and requirements. Some of the points in the exercises will be covered in the text either before or after the exercise. You might prefer to read each section right through before going back to tackle the exercises. Suggested answers are provided in italics after some of the exercises, so avoid these if you prefer to work through the exercises on your own. The aim is to prompt you to reflect on the material, remember what you have read and remind you to add your own thoughts. Space is provided for you to write your responses down in a few words, or you may prefer to just think about them. However, writing will help you to slow down and digest the material and may also enable you to process the information at a deeper level of understanding.

Finally, the overall aim of this Part is to direct you to the key points for academic and personal development. The twin emphases of academic development and personal qualities are stressed throughout. By giving attention to these factors you will give yourself the toolkit you will need to excel in your studies.

3.2	
dealing with theory	

This chapter will help you to:

- Recognise the importance of engaging with social theory
- Display the ability to think critically about 'social theory'
- Be able to test theories against six criteria.

Criminology is a theoretical discipline, and therefore you will be expected to be able to engage more generally with 'social theory'. As you will already be aware, criminologists will often hold differing opinions about where criminology should be most closely connected. Some undergraduate criminology programmes are delivered in departments of Law, Sociology, Social Policy or Political Studies. I see criminology as a social science that is closely allied with sociology, and I believe that criminology cannot be separated from social theory, as it is undoubtedly concerned with problems of social order and disorder. A look at the classic texts that influence criminology, for example, Marx, Durkheim, the Chicago School, clearly shows the way that criminology and social theory are deeply interwoven. I therefore believe that it is imperative that students of criminology are able to engage with and understand social theory. To that end, and to assist you in developing as a criminologist, I intend to begin by giving you some guidance about how to deal with 'theory' generally, and more specifically how you can go about 'evaluating' and thinking critically about social theory.

Six criteria for evaluating theory

It is not the case that to achieve success in criminology you must simply passively learn information and learn to repeat what you have been told. Instead, most courses will expect students to develop 'critical insight' or 'critical thinking'. This does not mean that they want or expect students to readily criticise everything that they encounter, rather they want them to consider the information that they receive, and consider what is good and what is bad, that they use the evidence and arguments that they encounter to form opinions, and that they use evidence to support assertions that they make. Essentially what is meant by these terms is that students are expected to have a comprehensive and informed knowledge, where opinions are formed by understanding drawn from a range of sources.

To help you develop critical thinking skills in criminology you will have to show that you can critique and scrutinise theory. To that end you might want to use the criteria presented below to assist you. You do not have to take a criminological theory and subject it to each criteria as a test, but rather regard these criteria as a set of guidelines that you can choose from when you encounter theory. They are intended to help you to display an ability to analyse and offer insightful comment, for example, you might talk about the potential applicability of biological criminology, such as eugenics or genetic engineering.

Criteria 1 – Logical consistency

Logical consistency is about whether a theory makes sense, essentially, is it clear? This means asking questions such as: Does a theory use clearly defined concepts? Does it use clearly defined relationships between concepts? (We call these propositions.) Essentially, does it make sense?

Criteria 2 – Scope

The concept of scope refers to whether there is clarity about the range of events, trends or facts that the theory intends to explain. For example, is it a theory that seeks to explain all crime, just some types of crimes, or perhaps only one type of crime? Is it a theory that applies in different places (perhaps one town, city or country)? For example, Robert Merton's concept of criminal innovation in 'strain theory' only really deals with crime which is financially motivated, and not all crime is.

Criteria 3 – Parsimony

The term parsimony literally means thriftiness or stinginess, but here it is used to make the assertion that any theoretical explanation should be as well-organised and well-argued as possible. The theory should not use more concepts and propositions than are necessary. The idea is that theory should use as few propositions as possible in order to explain the widest range of occurrence.

Criteria 4 – Testability

A theory must be tested against facts. It is not scientific if it cannot be 'verified' or 'falsified' by appropriate reportable and observable evidence. To describe this reportable and observable evidence, we use the term 'empirical'. A theory must be framed in such a way that its propositions are 'falsifiable' – meaning it must be possible, in principal, to prove it wrong. In criminology a good theory is one that is not proven wrong, as social scientists think it impossible to prove something 'absolutely true'.

Any theory, even if the evidence seems to fit, is only ever 'provisionally true'. This is as close as social scientists get to verification. A better theory or a better understanding and interpretation of the perceived facts may one day supersede it. This is especially true in social sciences!

Criteria 5 – Empirical validity

Empirical validity is concerned with whether a theory is supported by research evidence. If it is not, is it making grand claims with no evidence, or is it a hypothesis that needs further consideration? If it is based upon research we need to consider carefully how the research was gathered. Did more than one researcher produce the research? In more than one place? Was the research process undertaken over time or all at once? We need to consider whether the core principles that inform the research are falsified/proven wrong. Just because a theory isn't supported or tested empirically doesn't make it a bad theory (there are a number of criminological theories that cannot be empirically tested) but may serve to limit its usefulness in terms of application (see below).

Criteria 6 – Usefulness and applicability

I use this term because, as stated earlier, criminological theory can underpin, and be used to inform, criminal justice policy, interventions and practices. This criteria is concerned with describing how easily the theory can be turned into criminal justice policy and practice, but criminal justice policy-making is not simply based on rational, i.e. good, empirically grounded theory. It is likely to be based on a mix of ideological, cultural, economic and political considerations.

Moral principles and beliefs about how people should treat one another, for example, how society should treat offenders, should inform and influence the development of criminal justice policy. We should not be wholly influenced by what is effective and what seems to work, and policy and practice should not be determined by evidence of effectiveness alone. As an extreme example, if we found that cutting peoples limbs off, or executing them for theft worked better than anything else, we might still want to argue that it is not morally the correct thing to do.

Having begun to think about critically considering the theoretical material that you will encounter on your criminology course, It is now time to turn our attention to how, practically, you can make the most of the opportunities that are presented to you during undergraduate study. The following sections are intended as a guide to how you can achieve more from your study.

3.3

how to get the most out of your lectures

This chapter will help you to:

- Make the most of your lecture notes
- Prepare your mind for new terms
- Develop an independent approach to learning
- Write efficient summary notes from lectures
- Take the initiative in building on your lectures.

Keeping in context

According to higher educational commentators and advisors, best quality learning is facilitated when it is set within an overall learning context. It should be the responsibility of your tutors to provide a context for you to learn in, but it is also your responsibility to contribute to this overall environment, and you can do this even before your first lecture begins.

You can, and should develop an overview of the subject matter before you ever attend a lecture, and preparing adequately for lectures is the first way to ensure that you get the most out of them. This can be achieved by becoming familiar with the outline content of a given subject and the entire study programme. Before you go into each lecture you should briefly remind yourself of where it fits into the overall scheme of things. Think, for example, of how more confident you feel when you move into a new city (e.g. to attend university) once you become familiar with your surroundings, i.e. where you live in relation to college, shops, stores, stations, places of entertainment etc.

The same principle applies to your course – find your way around your study programme and try to figure out how it fits within the overall framework. Often course tutors provide module guidelines, you should always read these as they will not only help you to get a feel for the course, but they often also set out the tutors' expectations.

Use of lecture notes

It is always beneficial to do some preliminary reading before you enter a lecture. If lecture notes are provided in advance (for example, electronically), then print these out, read over them and bring them with you to the lecture. You can insert question marks on issues where you will need further clarification. Some lecturers prefer to provide full notes, some prefer to make skeleton outlines available and some prefer to issue no notes at all! If notes are provided, take full advantage and supplement these with your own notes as you listen. In a later section on memory techniques (see Chapter 3.6) you will see that humans possess ability for 're-learning savings', i.e. it is easier to learn material the second time round, as it is evident that we have a capacity to hold residual memory deposits. So some basic preparation will equip you with a great advantage – you will be able to 'tune in' and think more clearly about the lecture than you would have done without the preliminary work.

You ought to spend some time thinking about how and why you go about making lecture notes. What purpose will they serve? I would suggest that they are often best used as a means of navigating the subject on your own. If you take down everything said in a lecture you may not get the most from it. I always suggest that students make pertinent notes, such as author's names and any books mentioned. I would suggest that this will almost certainly be the case if notes are supplied to accompany the lecture.

Mastering technical terms

Let us assume that in an early lecture you are introduced to a series of new terms such as 'paradigm', 'recidivism', 'empirical' and 'hegemony'. If you are hearing these and other terms for the first time, you could end up with a headache! New words can be threatening, especially if you have to face a string of them in one lecture. The uncertainty about the new terms may impair your ability to benefit fully from the lecture and therefore hinder the quality of your learning. Some subjects require technical terms and the use of them is unavoidable. However, when you have heard a term a number of times it will not seem as daunting as it initially was.

In terms of learning new words, it will be very useful if you can work out what they mean from their context when you first encounter them. You might be much better at this than you imagine, especially if there is only one word in the sentence that you do not understand. It would also be very useful if you could obtain a small indexed notebook and use this to build up your own glossary of terms. In this way you could include a definition of a word, an example of its use, where it fits into a theory and any practical application of it.

To develop your learning it is worth investing some time in developing your vocabulary. To this end you should buy a good dictionary (this will also help you when you encounter terms you are unsure of). To progress in your study of criminology I would also suggest purchasing a dictionary of sociology, which are reasonably priced and offer definitions of many of the core terms you will encounter in criminology. Similarly McLaughlin and Muncie's (2001) Sage Dictionary of Criminology *is also a useful resource.*

Remember you can also extend your vocabulary by reading a broad range of material that will help you to learn new words, and this may improve your ability to write generally. Reading broadsheet newspapers, for example, will benefit you two-fold: It will assist you in developing your writing, while it will also extend your knowledge of the practices of the criminal justice system that will form the backdrop to academic criminology.

Checklist: Mastering terms used in your lectures

✓ Read lecture notes before the lectures and list any unfamiliar terms
✓ Read over the listed terms until you are familiar with their sound
✓ Try to work out meanings of terms from their context
✓ Write out a sentence that includes the new word (do this for each word)
✓ Meet with other students and test each other with the technical terms
✓ Note down any new words that you hear in lectures and check out the meaning soon afterwards
✓ Do not be afraid to ask if you do not understand something.

Note-taking strategy

Note-taking in lectures is an art that you will only perfect with practise and by trial and error. You should not feel that you cannot ignore my opinions if you find an alternative formula that works best for you. What works for one, does not always work for all. Some students can write more quickly than others, some are better at short hand than others and some are better at deciphering their own scrawl! The problem will always be to try to find a balance between concentrating beneficially on what you hear, and making sufficient notes that will enable you to later comprehend what you have heard. You should not, however, become frustrated by the fact that you will not immediately understand or remember everything you have heard.

By being present at a lecture you will already have an advantage over students that do not attend. The notes that you take will undoubtedly benefit you further, but I would urge you to consider why you take notes and how you will use them. By stopping and asking yourself this, and reflecting on it, it is likely that you will produce more useful notes.

Some guidelines for note-taking in lectures

• Develop the note-taking strategy that works best for you
• Work at finding a balance between listening and writing
• Make some use of optimal short hand (for example, a few key words may summarise a story)
• Too much writing may impair the flow of the lecture for you

- Too much writing may impair the quality of your notes
- Some limited notes are better than none
- Good note-taking may facilitate deeper processing of information
- It is essential to 'tidy up' notes as soon as possible after a lecture
- Reading over notes soon after lectures will consolidate your learning.

Developing the lecture

Lectures are not just a passive experience

- *Try to interact with the lecture material by asking questions*
- *Highlight points that you would like to develop in personal study*
- *Trace connections between the lecture and other parts of your study programme*
- *Bring together notes from the lecture and other sources*
- *Restructure the lecture outline into your own preferred format*
- *Think of ways in which aspects of the lecture material can be applied*
- *Design ways in which aspects of the lecture material can be illustrated*
- *If the lecturer invites questions, make a note of all the questions asked*
- *Follow up on issues of interest that have arisen out of the lecture.*

3.4

how to get the most out of your seminars

This chapter will help you to:

- Be aware of the value of seminars
- Focus on links to learning
- Recognise qualities you can use repeatedly
- Manage potential problems in seminars
- Prepare yourself adequately for seminars.

Not to be under-estimated

Seminars are often optional in a degree programme and sometimes poorly attended because they are under-estimated. Some students may be convinced that the lecture is the truly authoritative way to receive quality information. Undoubtedly, lectures play an important role in an academic programme, but seminars have a unique contribution to learning that will complement lectures. Other students may feel that their time would be better spent in personal study. Again, private study is unquestionably essential for personal learning and development, but you will nevertheless diminish your learning experience if you neglect seminars. If seminars were to be removed from academic programmes, then something really important would be lost.

An asset to complement other learning activities

Seminars will provide you with a unique opportunity to learn and develop. At university, it is in seminars that you will hear a variety of contributions, and different perspectives and emphases. You will have the chance to interrupt and the experience of being interrupted! You will also learn that you can get things wrong! It is often the case that when one student admits that they did not know some important piece of information, other students quickly follow on to the same admission in the wake of this. If you can learn to ask questions and not feel stupid, then seminars will give you an asset for learning and a life-long educational quality.

Creating the right climate in seminars

In lectures your main role is to listen and take notes, but in seminars there is the challenge to strike the balance between listening and speaking. It is important to make a beginning in speaking even if it is just to repeat something that you agree with. However, seminars are only one aspect of the learning process. If you are committed to independent learning you will have more to offer other students if you work in small groups, and you will also be prompted to follow up on the leads given by them. Furthermore, the guidelines given to you in lectures are designed to lead you into deeper independent study. The issues raised in lectures are pointers to provide direction and structure for your extended personal pursuit. Your aim should invariably be to build on what you are given, and you should never think of merely returning the bare bones of the lecture material in a course work essay or exam.

> *It almost never fails to impress tutors and markers if you show a contemporary knowledge of the subject that expands upon the content of the course and shows an ability to gather evidence beyond the material covered in the course. Use journals to search for relevant studies that may be cited in exams and essays.*

Links in learning and transferable skills

An important principle in the progression from shallow to deep learning is developing the capacity to make connecting links between themes or topics and across subjects. This also applies to the various learning activities such as lectures, seminars, fieldwork, computer searches and private study. Another factor to think about is, 'What skills can I develop, or improve on, from seminars that I can use across my study programme?' A couple of examples of key skills are the ability to communicate and the capacity to work within a team. These are skills that you will be able to use at various points in your course (they are transferable), but you are not likely to develop them within the formal setting of a lecture.

> *It is worth remembering that these skills are also transferable to the world of work, and many of the skills that you will use at university will be highly sought after by employers. Think about how what you have done at university might mirror skills that employers may ask for.*

> *In each criminology seminar that you attend you should be looking for links between subjects and the broader themes. If you are studying a module-based course, it is likely that topics covered in some modules will link and compliment other modules. Look for these links to maximise the value of each and every seminar.*

An opportunity to contribute

If you have never made a contribution to a seminar before, you may need something to use as an 'ice breaker'. It does not matter if your first contribution is only a sentence or two – the important thing is to make a start. One way to do this is to make brief notes as others contribute, and whilst doing this a question or two might arise in your mind. If your first contribution is a question, that is a good start. Or it may be that you will be able to point out some connection between what others have said, or identify conflicting opinions that need to be resolved. If you have already begun making contributions, it is important that you keep the momentum going, and do not allow yourself to lapse back into the safe cocoon of shyness.

Strategies for benefiting from your seminar experience

If you are required to do a presentation in your seminar, you might want to consult a full chapter on presentations in a complementary study guide (for example, McIlroy, 2003). Alternatively, you may be content with the summary bullet points presented as a checklist below. In order to benefit from discussions in seminars (the focus of this chapter), the following may be useful.

Checklist: How to benefit from seminars

✓ Do some preparatory reading
✓ Familiarise yourself with the main ideas to be addressed
✓ Make notes during the seminar
✓ Make some verbal contribution, even a question
✓ Remind yourself of the skills you can develop
✓ Trace learning links from the seminar to other subjects/topics on your programme
✓ Make brief bullet points on what you should follow up
✓ Read over your notes as soon as possible after the seminar
✓ Continue discussion with fellow students after the seminar has ended.

3.5

essay writing tips

This chapter will help you to:

- Quickly engage with the main arguments
- Channel your passions constructively
- Note your main arguments in an outline
- Find and focus on your central topic questions
- Weave quotations into your essay.

Getting into the flow

In essay writing one of your first aims should be to get your mind active and engaged with your subject. A former teacher of mine used to say 'practice makes better!' which I find a good tonic to the idea that 'perfection' is attainable. Just as professional sportspeople will practise their skills, and 'warm up' before an event, you can 'warm up' for your essay. Practice will make you better, and reflecting on ideas in your head before you begin to write, will allow you to think within the framework of your topic, and this will be especially important if you are coming to the subject for the first time.

The tributary principle

A tributary is a stream that runs into a main river as it wends its way to the sea. Similarly in an essay you should ensure that every idea you introduce is moving toward the overall theme you are addressing. Your idea might of course be relevant to a subheading that is in turn relevant to a main heading. Every idea you introduce is to be a 'feeder' into the flowing theme. In addition to tributaries, there can also be 'distributaries', which are streams that flow away from the river. In an essay, these would represent the ideas that run away from the main stream of thought and leave the reader trying to work out what their relevance may have been. It is one thing to have grasped your subject thoroughly, but quite another to convince your reader that this is the case. Your aim should be to build up ideas sentence-by-sentence and paragraph-by-paragraph, until you have communicated your clear purpose to the reader.

> *It is important in essay writing that you do not include material that is irrelevant. It is also important that you make linking statements – these will convey to the reader that you have made the link. Also, explain how what you are using contributes to your discussion and why it is relevant.*

Listing and linking the key concepts

All subjects will have central concepts that can sometimes be usefully labelled by a single word. Course textbooks may include a glossary of terms and these provide a direct route to the beginning of efficient mastery of the topic. The central words or terms are the essential raw materials that you will need to build upon. Ensure that you learn the words and their definitions, and that you can go on to link the key words together, so that in your learning activities you will add understanding. The glossary in this book should help you toward this goal.

“ How can punishment be justified? ”

You might decide to draft your outline in the following manner, or you may prefer to use a mind map approach. (This is not necessarily how you *should* answer such a question, but provides some pointers.)

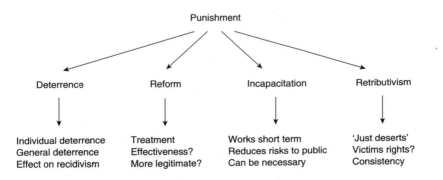

Deterrence	Reform	Incapacitation	Retributivism
Individual deterrence General deterrence Effect on recidivism	Treatment Effectiveness? More legitimate?	Works short term Reduces risks to public Can be necessary	'Just deserts' Victims rights? Consistency

An adversarial system

In higher education students are required to make the transition from descriptive to critical writing. If you can think of the critical approach as a law case that is being conducted where there is both a prosecution and a defence, your concern should be for objectivity, transparency and fairness. No matter how passionately you may feel about a given cause you must not allow information to be filtered out because of your personal prejudice. An essay is not to become a crusade for a cause in which the contrary arguments are not addressed in an evenhanded manner. This means that you should show awareness that opposite views are held and you should at least represent these as accurately as possible.

In many ways your role as a writer is to play judge; you assess all the evidence presented, and then come to a decision on that basis. That is not too say that you cannot have an opinion or make a conclusion that you feel is appropriate, but you must give both sides of an argument a fair hearing!

Stirring up passions

The above points do not of course mean that you are not entitled to personal persuasion or to feel passionately about your subject. On the contrary, such feelings may well be a marked advantage if you can bring them under control and channel them into balanced, effective writing (see example below). Some students may be struggling at the other end of the spectrum – being required to write about a topic that they feel quite indifferent about. As you engage with your topic and toss the ideas around in your mind, you will hopefully find that your interest is stimulated, if only at an intellectual level initially. How strongly you feel about a topic or how much you are interested in it, may depend on whether you choose the topic yourself or whether it has been given to you as an obligatory assignment.

An example of an issue that may stir up passions

Should a sentence of life imprisonment for murder mean life?

For	Against
• It would be a strong form of 'incapacitation'	• There is no proof of deterrent effect, as many murders would still happen
• The general deterrent effect	• Miscarriages of justice can and do occur

- Individual deterrent effect
- Such sentences might provide justice for victims
- Freed life-sentenced prisoners have killed again
- There are already natural life prisoners in Britain
- By using utilitarian principles, it can be argued that the rights of the individual are outweighed by the greater good of the public who are being protected.

- Such a punishment could be unjust in implementation
- The existing system of life imprisonment is effective
- Prisoners serving natural life have 'nothing to lose' in prison
- Such a sentence panders to popular punitiveness
- The prison population would increase
- The resultant ageing prison population creates problems with regard a care/control balance, as it has in America.
- Such an approach gives no credit to the possibility of reform or treatment.

Structuring an outline

Whenever you sense a flow of inspiration to write on a given subject, it is essential that you put this into a structure that will allow your inspiration to be communicated clearly. It is a basic principle in all walks of life that structure and order facilitate good communication. Therefore, when you have the flow of inspiration in your essay you must get this into a structure that will allow the marker to recognise the true quality of your work. For example, you might plan for an introduction, conclusion, three main headings and each of these with several subheadings (see example overleaf). Moreover, you may decide not to include your headings in your final presentation, i.e. just use them initially to structure and balance your arguments. Once you have drafted this outline you can then easily sketch an introduction, and you will have been well prepared for the conclusion when you arrive at that point.

Common pitfall: Students who achieve lower marks often lack focus in their work, a good structure will help you to achieve a balance in the weight of each of your arguments, while a good essay plan will also support you toward this goal. Also remember that preparation is one vital aspect of presentation, but so is proof-reading and accuracy checking: you should spend a sizable time re-reading what you have written for presentation, grammar, clarity, accuracy etc.

Again it might be useful to attempt to write an essay, and therefore, the example below gives an outline structure that you could use to write a purposeful essay. The topic is one relevant to criminology and the authors named can be traced and read if you want to practise researching and writing an essay. Again this is only one approach that you could take (there is never a right answer).

❝'when you enter the mind of a murderer, you approach with caution. There is an understandable concern with what you might find there' (Cullen and Newell, 1999). When the minds of serial killers are entered, can plausible explanations for why they have killed be found?❞

1. *Defining Serial Murder*

    a. Defining serial murder is very complex and contested (Coleman and Norris, 2000)

    b. We may know very little as to the extent of such a phenomenon (Kiger, 1990)

    c. Serial murder may be increasing, and this may be due to social influences and factors (Leyton, 1989)

    d. We have a duty to try to find explanations; and these may assist in locating and identifying perpetrators.

2. *Explanations for Serial Murder*

Holmes and DeBurger (1988) and Holmes and Holmes (1998) offer four typologies:

    a. Visionary (describe)

    b. Missionary

    c. Hedonistic

    d. Power/control.

3. *Other Factors – Biological*

    a. Genetic factors

    b. Head trauma

    c. Abnormal brain activity

4. *Other Factors – Psychological*

    a. Psychosis (Hickey, 1997)

    b. Psychopath (Hare, 1993)

5. *Other Factors – Sociological*

   Leyton (1989)

6. *Conclusion*

   Which explanations are convincing (if any)? Why are they convincing?

Selecting pertinent topics

When you are constructing a draft outline for an essay or project, you should ask what the major question(s) are that you wish to address, or which topics and subjects are pertinent to the subject. It would be useful to make a list of all the issues that spring to mind that you might wish to tackle. The ability to design a good question is an art form that should be cultivated, and such questions will allow you to impress your assessor with the quality of your thinking.

   To illustrate the point, consider the example presented below. If you were asked to write an essay about the effectiveness of the police in your local community you might, as your starting point, pose the following questions.

The effectiveness of the police in the local community: Initial questions

- Is there a high profile police presence?
- Are there regular 'on the beat' officers and patrol car activities?
- Do recent statistics show increases or decreases in crime in the area?
- Are the police involved in community activities and local schools?
- Does the local community welcome and support the police?
- Do the police have a good reputation for responding to calls?
- Do the police harass people unnecessarily?
- Do minority groups perceive the police as fair?
- Do the police have an effective complaints procedure to deal with grievances against them?
- Do the police solicit and respond to local community concerns?

Rest your case

It should be your aim to give the clear impression that your arguments are not based entirely on hunches, bias, feelings or intuition. In exams and essay questions it is usually assumed (even if not directly specified) that you will appeal to evidence to support your claims. Therefore, when you write your essay, you should ensure that it is liberally sprinkled with citations and evidence. By the time the assessor reaches the end of your work, he or she should be convinced that your conclusions are evidence-based. A fatal flaw to be avoided is to make claims for which you have provided no authoritative source.

You should convey a clear impression that what you have asserted is derived from relevant sources (including sources that are up to date). It looks better in terms of presentation if you spread your citations across your essay rather than compressing them into a paragraph or two at the end. Indeed if you are looking to show knowledge that has been gained through wider reading and study, you should produce an essay that is punctuated with citations. Good examples of presentation can be found in academic journals.

Some examples of how you might introduce your evidence and sources are provided below:

According to Young (1999) ...
Garland (2002) has concluded that ...
Taylor (1999) found that ...
It has been claimed by Wilson and O'Sullivan (2004) that ...
Messerschmidt (1993) has asserted that ...
A review of the evidence by McGuire and Priestley (1995) suggests that ...

It is sensible to vary the expression used so that you are not monotonous and repetitive, and it also aids variety to introduce researcher's names at various places in the sentence (not always at the beginning). It is advisable to choose the expression that is most appropriate – for example, you can make a stronger statement about reviews that have identified recurrent and predominant trends in findings as opposed to one study that appears to run contrary to all the rest.

Careful use of quotations

Although it is desirable to present a good range of cited sources, it is not judicious to present these as a 'patchwork quilt', i.e. you just paste together what others have said with little thought for interpretative comment or coherent structure. It is a good general point to aim to avoid very lengthy quotes – short ones can be very effective. Aim at blending the quotations as naturally as possible into the flow of your sentences. Also, it is good to vary your practices – sometimes use short, direct, brief quotes (cite page number as well as author and year), and at times you can summarise the gist of a quote in your own words. In this case you should cite the author's name and year of publication but leave out quotation marks and page number.

In terms of referencing, practice may vary from one discipline to the next, but some general points that will go a long way in contributing to good practice are as follows:

- If a reference is cited in the text, it must be in the list at the end (and vice-versa)
- Names and dates in the text should correspond exactly with the list in your References or Bibliography
- The list of References and Bibliography should be in alphabetical order by the surname (not the initials) of the author or first author
- Any reference you make in the text should be traceable by the reader (they should clearly be able to identify and trace the source)
- Accurate referencing is important, and failure to accurately reference can impact upon your marks
- Every institution will have guidelines available, and seeking these out will help you appreciate the accepted convention for your course.

A clearly defined introduction

In an introduction to an essay you have the opportunity to define the problem or issue that is being addressed and to set it within context. Resist the temptation to elaborate on any issue at the introductory stage. What you should aim to do at the introduction is to provide an essence of what will follow in order to set a context. To this end, it is far better to be succinct and leave the reader wanting to read further.

EXERCISE

An example for practice, if you wish, can be engaged if you look back at the drafted outline on serial killers (pages 144–145). Try to design an introduction for that essay in about three or four sentences.

Conclusion – adding the finishing touches

In the conclusion you should aim to tie your essay together in a clear and coherent manner. It is your last chance to leave an overall impression in your reader's mind. Therefore, you will at this stage want to do justice to your efforts and not sell yourself short. This is your opportunity to identify where the strongest evidence points or where the balance of probability lies. The conclusion to an exam question often has to be written hurriedly under the pressure of time, but with an essay (coursework) you have time to reflect on, refine and adjust the content to your satisfaction. It should be your goal to make the conclusion a smooth finish that does justice to the range of content in summary and succinct form. Do not under-estimate the value of an effective conclusion. 'Sign off' your essay in a manner that brings closure to the treatment of your subject.

Top down and bottom up clarity

An essay gives you the opportunity to refine each sentence and paragraph on your computer. Each sentence is like a tributary that leads into the stream of the paragraph that in turn leads into the mainstream of the essay. From a 'top down' perspective (i.e. starting at the top with your major outline points), clarity is facilitated by the structure you draft in your outline. You can ensure that the subheadings are appropriately placed under the most relevant main heading, and that both sub and main headings are arranged in logical sequence. From a 'bottom up' perspective (i.e. building up the details that 'flesh out' your main points), you should check that each sentence is a 'feeder' for the predominant concept in a given paragraph. When all this is done you can check that the transition from one point to the next is smooth rather than abrupt.

Checklist: Summary for essay writing

✓ Before you start, have a 'warm up' by tossing the issues around in your head

✓ List the major concepts and link them in fluent form

✓ Design a structure (outline) that will facilitate balance, progression, fluency and clarity

✓ Pose questions and address these in critical fashion

✓ Demonstrate that your arguments rest on evidence and spread cited sources across your essay

✓ Provide an introduction that sets the scene and a conclusion that rounds off the arguments.

Checklist: Attempt to write (or at least think about) some additional features that would help facilitate good essay writing:

✓ ....

✓ ....

✓ ....

✓ ....

✓ ....

In the above checklist your could have features such as originality, clarity in sentence and paragraph structure, applied aspects, addressing a subject you feel passionately about and the ability to avoid going off on a tangent.

3.6	
revision hints and tips	

This chapter will help you to:

- Map out your accumulated material for revision
- Choose summary tags to guide your revision
- Keep well-organised folders for revision
- Make use of effective memory techniques
- Revise in a way that combines bullet points and in-depth reading
- Profit from the benefits of revising with others
- Attend to the practical exam details that will help keep panic at bay
- Use strategies that keep you task-focused during the exam
- Select and apply relevant points from your prepared outlines.

Start at the beginning

Strategy for revision should be on your mind from your first lecture at the beginning of your academic semester. You should be like the squirrel that stores up nuts for the winter. Do not waste any lecture, tutorial, seminar, group discussion etc. by letting the material evaporate into thin air. Get into the habit of making a few guidelines for revision after each learning activity. Keep a folder, or file, or little notebook that is reserved for revision and write out the major points that you have learned. By establishing this regular practice you will find that what you have learned becomes consolidated in your mind, and you will also be in a better position to 'import' and 'export' your material both within and across subjects.

Compile summary notes

It would be useful and convenient to have a little notebook or cards on which you can write outline summaries that provide you with an over-view of your subject at a glance. You could also use treasury tags to hold different batches of cards together whilst still allowing for inserts and re-sorting. Such practical resources can easily be slipped into your pocket or bag and produced when you are on the bus or train or whilst sitting in a traffic jam. They would also be useful if you are standing in a queue or waiting for someone who is not in a rush! A glance over your notes will consolidate your learning and will also activate your mind to think further about your subject. Therefore it would also be useful to make note of the questions that you would like to think about in greater depth. Your primary task is to get into the habit of constructing outline notes that will be useful for revision.

Keep organised records

People who have a fulfilled career have usually developed the twin skills of time and task management. It is worth pausing to remember that you can use your academic training to prepare for your future career in this respect. Therefore, ensure that you do not fall short of your potential because these qualities have not been cultivated. One important tactic is to keep a folder for each subject and divide this topic-by-topic. You can keep your topics in the same order in which they are presented in your course lectures. Bind them together in a ring binder or folder and use subject dividers to keep them apart. Make a numbered list of the contents at the beginning of the folder, and list each topic clearly as it marks a new section in your folder. Another important practice is to place all your notes on a given topic within the appropriate section and don't put off this simple task, do it straightaway. Notes may come from lectures, seminars, tutorials, internet searches, personal notes etc. It is also essential that when you remove these for consultation, you return them to their 'home' immediately after use.

The most important point here is that you will have gathered a wide variety of material that should be organised in such a way that will allow you to use a range of evidence to come up with some satisfactory and authoritative conclusions. Being organised will help you toward your end goal, whereas poor organisation will hinder you.

Use past papers

Revision will be very limited if it is confined to memory work. You should, by all means, read over your revision cards or notebook and keep the picture of the major facts in front of your mind's eye. It is also, however, essential that you become familiar with previous exam papers so that you will have some idea of how the questions are likely to be framed. Therefore, build up a good range of past exam papers (especially recent ones) and add these to your folder.

It is very unlikely that in examinations the questions that you are asked will be abstract, or cover a subject in a wholly different way, though it is possible that this may be the case. You can prepare yourself mentally, to a degree, by running over what you might be asked in your mind, and thinking about how best you might answer. Such a trick is a transferable skill that you can also apply to job interviews!

" Evaluate the advantages and disadvantages of Prison Privatisation. (Note: this should not be seen as an extensive list but rather as an example of some of the issues.) "

Immediately you can see that you will require two lists and you can begin to work on documenting your reasons under each, as below:

Advantages	Disadvantages
• The introduction of private sector competition improves standards in state sector prisons	• The state arrests and prosecutes, and therefore also has a moral responsibility to punish
• Private prisons provide an effective means of increasing the prison capacity	• Pay and conditions in private prisons compare unfavourably with state run prisons, and this has 'knock on' effects in terms of staff quality
• The need for more flexibility on the part of prison staff	• Private prisons experience more control problems and disorder than state prisons
• Substantially reduced costs	• In the long term, private prisons are no more profitable
• Economically free competition in the market place spurs efficiency and quality of service	• Private prisons having a desire to make profit; can provide less in terms of staff, regimes etc.
• Prison privatisation reduced the power of the Prison Officers association, which had previously been too militant	• Building private prisons commits the state to expanding the prison population, rather than finding other effective solutions.

You will have also noticed that the word 'evaluate' is in the question – so your mind must go to work on making judgements. You may decide to work through disadvantages first and then through advantages or it may be your preference to compare, point by point, as you go along. Whatever conclusion you come to may be down to personal, subjective opinion but at least you will have worked through all the issues from both standpoints. The lesson is to ensure that part of your revision should include critical thinking as well as memory work.

Employ effective mnemonics (memory aids)

The Greek word from which 'mnemonics' is derived refers to a tomb – a structure that is built in memory of a loved one, friend or respected person. 'Mnemonics' can be simply defined as aids to memory – devices that will help you recall information that might otherwise be difficult to retrieve from memory. For example, if you find an old toy in the attic of your house, it may suddenly trigger a flood of childhood memories associated with it. Mnemonics can therefore be thought of as keys that open your memory's storehouse.

Visualisation is one technique that can be used to aid memory. For example, the **location method** is where a familiar journey is visualised and you can 'place' the facts that you wish to remember at various landmarks along the journey, for example, a bus stop, a car park, a shop, a store, a bend, a police station, a traffic light etc. This has the advantage of making an association of the information you have to learn with other material that is already firmly embedded and structured in your memory. Therefore, once the relevant memory is activated, a dynamic 'domino effect' will be triggered. However, there is no reason why you cannot use a whole toolkit of mnemonics. As well as the location method defined above, some other examples and illustrations of mnemonics are presented below.

Visualisation – turn information into pictures. Some people find that their memory is stimulated by visualising an image, an example might be to read Lombroso's *Criminal Man* (1876) and try to visualise a picture of what such a criminal might look like; remember the features of atavism that Lombroso sets out. You may then be able to recall more than if you tried just to read and memorise text.

Peg system – 'Hang' information onto a term so that when you hear the term you will remember the ideas connected with it (an umbrella term). In the example on typologies of serial killers there are four different types: visionary, missionary, hedonistic and power control. Under visionary you could remember key features of this type, e.g. hallucinations, inner voices, random victim selection, disorganisation.

Hierarchical system – This is a development of the previous point with higher-order, middle-order and lower-order terms. For example, you could think of the continents of the world (higher order), and then group these into the countries under them (middle order). Under countries you could then have cities, rivers and mountains (lower order).

Acronyms – Take the first letter of all the key words and make a word from these, some people find this a useful aid to memory. In criminology and criminal justice studies acronyms are quite frequently used, for example, the anti-social behaviour order becomes the ASBO.

Mind maps – These have become very popular – they allow you to draw lines that stretch out from the central idea and to develop the subsidiary ideas in the same way. It is a little like the pegging and hierarchical methods combined and turned sideways! The method has the advantage of giving you the complete picture at a glance, although they can become a complex work of art!

Rhymes – words that rhyme and words that end with a similar sound (e.g. commemoration, celebration, anticipation). These provide another dimension to memory work by including sound. Memory can be enhanced when information is processed in various modalities, for example, hearing, seeing, speaking, visualising.

Alternate between methods

It is not sufficient to present outline points in response to an exam question (although it is better to do this than nothing if you have run out of time in your exam). Your aim should be to put 'meat on the bones' by adding substance, evidence and arguments to your basic points. You should work at finding the balance between the two methods – outline revision cards might be best reserved for short bus journeys, whereas extended reading might be better employed for longer revision slots at home or in the library. Your ultimate goal should be to bring together an effective, working approach that will enable you to face your exam questions comprehensively and confidently.

Revising with others

If you can find a few other students to revise with, this will provide another fresh approach to the last stages of your learning. First ensure that others carry their work load and are not merely using the hard work of others as a short cut to success. Of course you should think of group sessions as one method, but it is not the only method. A collective approach will allow you to assess your strengths and weaknesses (showing you where you are off track), and to benefit from the resources and insights of others, but some people *do* revise more effectively on their own, without distractions. If you do revise with others, try to design some questions for the whole group to address before you meet. It is also worth making this a task for other group members. The group could also go through past exam papers and discuss the points that might provide an effective response to each question. It should not be the aim of the group to provide standard and identical answers for each group member to mimic. Group work is currently deemed to be advantageous by educationalists, and team work is held to be a desirable employability quality.

Checklist: Good study habits for revision time

✓ Set a date for the 'official' beginning of revision and prepare for 'revision mode'
✓ Do not force cramming by leaving revision too late
✓ Take breaks from revision to avoid saturation
✓ Indulge in relaxing activities to give your mind a break from pressure
✓ Minimise or eliminate use of alcohol during the revision season
✓ Get into a good rhythm of sleep to allow renewal of your mind
✓ Avoid excessive caffeine especially at night so that sleep is not disrupted
✓ Try to adhere to regular eating patterns
✓ Try to have a brisk walk in fresh air each day (for example, in the park)
✓ Avoid excessive dependence on junk food and snacks.

3.7	
exam tips	

This chapter will help you to:

• Develop strategies for controlling your nervous energy
• Tackle worked examples of time and task management in exams
• Attend to the practical details associated with the exam
• Stay focused on the exam questions
• Link revision outlines to strategy for addressing exam questions.

Handling your nerves

Exam nerves are not unusual and it has been concluded that test anxiety arises because of the perception that your performance is being evaluated, that the consequences are likely to be serious and that you are working under the pressure of a time restriction. However, it has also been asserted that the activation of the Autonomic Nervous System is adaptive in that is designed to prompt us to take action in order to avoid danger. If you focus on the task at hand rather than on feeding a downward negative spiral in your thinking patterns, this will help you keep your nerves under control. In the run up to your exams you can practice some simple relaxation techniques that will help you bring stress under control.

Practices that may help reduce or buffer the effects of exam stress

- Listening to music
- Going for a brisk walk
- Simple breathing exercises
- Some muscle relaxation
- Watching a movie
- Enjoying some laughter
- Doing some exercise
- Relaxing in a bath (with music if preferred).

The best choice is going to be the one (or combination) that works best for you – perhaps to be discovered by trial and error. Some of the above techniques can be practised on the morning of the exam, and even the memory of them can be used just before the exam. For example, you could run over a relaxing tune in your head, and have this echo inside you as you enter the exam room. The idea behind all this is, first, stress levels must come down, and second, relaxing thoughts will serve to displace stressful reactions. It has been said that stress is the body's call to take action, but anxiety is a maladaptive response to that call.

Time management with examples

The all-important matter as you approach an exam is to develop the belief that you can take control over the situation. As you work through the list of issues that you need to address, you will be able to tick them off one by one. One of the issues you will need to be clear about before the exam is the length of time you should allocate to each question. Sometimes this can be quite simple (although it is always necessary to read the rubric carefully), for example, if two questions are to be answered in a two hour paper, you should allow one hour for each question. If it is a two-hour paper with one essay question and 5 shorter answers, you could allow one hour for the essay and 12 minutes each for the shorter questions. However, you always need to check out the weighting for the marks on each question, and you will also need to deduct whatever time it takes you to read over the paper and to choose your questions.

Common pitfall: Too many students make basic mistakes in exams because they fail at the simplest of tasks. Remember to check the time limit on the paper, to allocate time accordingly between questions, and then stick to timings. Also, although it sounds like common sense, read the questions thoroughly and make sure that you are certain what you are being asked. Frequently students limit their marks by falling into common traps, do not allow yourself to make this mistake.

After you have decided on the questions you wish to address, you then need to plan your answers. Some students prefer to plan all outlines and draft work at the beginning, whilst others prefer to plan and address one answer before proceeding to address the next question. Decide on your strategy before you enter the exam room and stick to your plan. When you have done your draft outline as rough work, you should allocate an appropriate time for each section. This will prevent you from excessive treatment of some aspects whilst falling short on other parts. Such careful planning will help you achieve balance, fluency and symmetry.

Common pitfall: Some students put as much effort into their rough work as they do into their exam essay, but if this is not allowed to be marked, is there any purpose? These are issues where you must decide upon the necessary balance, and find the position where you feel adequately prepared given the time constraints. You do not want to limit your marks because too much time was spent on the plan.

EXERCISE

Workout the time allocation for the following outline allowing for one hour on the question. Deduct 10 minutes taken at the beginning for choice and planning.

(Continued)

(Continued)

Discuss whether it is justifiable to make fox-hunting criminal

1. *Arguments for criminalisation*

   a. Other type of 'cruelty' to animals are criminal
   b. The majority of the public dislike fox-hunting
   c. Criminalisation is the only effective means of showing society's disapproval and preventing hunting from taking place.

2. *Arguments against a ban*

   a. Many members of the public agree with hunting; and there is no reason to criminalise such behaviour
   b. Hunting is an effective means of regulating the fox population
   c. A ban would affect people's previously legitimate livelihoods.

3. *Qualifying suggestions*

   a. Regulated or sanctioned hunts
   b. Drag hunting (where live creatures are not chased).

Attend to practical details

This short section is designed to remind you of the practical details that should be attended to in preparation for an exam. There are always students who turn up late, or to the wrong venue or for the wrong exam, or do not turn up at all! Check and re-check that you have all the details of each exam correctly noted. What you don't need is to arrive late and then have to tame your panic reactions. The exam season is the time when you should aim to be at your best.

Common pitfall: Students frequently disadvantage themselves because of basic failures in adequate planning and preparation in terms of practical details.

Make note of the following details and check that you have taken control of each one.

Checklist: Practical exam details

✓ Check that you have the correct venue

✓ Make sure you know how to locate the venue before the exam day

✓ Ensure that the exam time you have noted is accurate

✓ Allow sufficient time for your journey and consider the possibility of delays

✓ Bring an adequate supply of stationary and include back up

✓ Bring a watch for your time and task management

✓ You may need some liquid such as a small bottle of still water

✓ You may also need to bring some tissues

✓ Observe whatever exam regulations your university/college has set in place

✓ Fill in required personal details before the exam begins.

Control wandering thoughts

When in your exams, try to keep to task. Again this may sound like common sense but it is true to suggest that 'one way you may fail your exam is to get up and walk out of the test room without writing anything', but another way is to 'leave' the test room mentally by being preoccupied with distracting thoughts. The distracting thoughts may be either related to the exam itself or totally irrelevant to it. The net effect of both these forms of intrusion is to distract you from the task at hand and debilitate your test performance.

Research has consistently shown that distracting, intrusive thoughts during an exam are more detrimental to performance than stressful symptoms such as sweaty palms, dry mouth, tension, trembling etc. Moreover, it does not matter whether the distracting thoughts are negative evaluations related to the exam or are totally irrelevant to the exam. The latter may be a form of escape from the stressful situation.

Practical suggestions for controlling wandering thoughts

• Be aware that this problem is detrimental to performance
• Do not look around to find distractions
• If distracted, write down 'keep focused on task'
• If distracted again, look back at your 'keep focused' instruction and continue to do this

- Start to draft rough work as soon as you can
- If you struggle with initial focus then re-read or elaborate on your rough work
- If you have started your essay re-read your last paragraph (or two)
- Do not throw fuel on your distracting thoughts – starve them by re-engaging with the task at hand.

Links to revision

If you have followed the guidelines given for revision, you will be well equipped with outline plans when you enter the exam room. You may have chosen to use headings and subheadings, mind maps, hierarchical approaches or just a series of simple mnemonics. Whatever method you choose to use, you should be furnished with a series of memory triggers that will trigger memory for you once you begin to write. You also might want to restrict your focus to, say, three or four subjects that you feel most comfortable and familiar with, although of course this will depend upon circumstance and what is required of you.

The art of 'name dropping'

In most topics at university you will be required to cite studies as evidence for your arguments and to link these to the names of researchers, scholars or theorists. It will help if you can use the correct dates or at least the decades, and it is good to demonstrate that you have used contemporary sources, and have done some independent work. A marker will have dozens if not hundreds of scripts to work through and they will know if you are just repeating the same phrases from the same sources as every one else. There is inevitably a certain amount of this that must go on, but there is room for you to add fresh and original touches that demonstrate independence and imagination.

> *Convey the impression that you have done more than the bear minimum and that you are enthusiastic about criminology. Like essay writing, use citations to support arguments (you may even be able to remember some brief quotations). There is no reason that an examination essay should adopt a format that is radically different to that of a written essay. Try to spread researcher's and theorists names across your exam essay rather than compressing them into, for example, the first and last paragraphs.*

Flight, fight or freeze

As previously noted, the Autonomic Nervous System (ANS) is activated when danger or apparent danger is imminent. Of course the threat does not have to be physical, as in the case of an exam, a job interview, a driving test or a TV appearance. Indeed the ANS can be activated even at the anticipation of a future threat. However, the reaction is more likely to be stronger as you enter into the crucial time of testing or challenge. Symptoms may include deep breathing, trembling, headaches, nausea, tension, dry mouth and palpitations. How should we react to these once they have been triggered? A postman might decide to run away from a barking dog and run the risk of being chased and bitten. A second possible response is to freeze on the spot – this might arrest the animal on its tracks, but is no use in an exam situation. In contrast, to fight might not be the best strategy against the dog, but will be more productive in an exam. That is, you are going into the exam room to 'tackle' the questions, and not to run away from the challenge before you.

A politician's answer

Politicians are renowned for refusing to answer questions directly or for evading them through raising other questions. A humorous example is when a politician was asked, 'Is it true that you always answer questions by asking another?' The reply given was, 'Who told you that?'

The message here is to make sure that you answer the set question, although there may be other questions that arise out of this for further study that you might want to highlight in your conclusion. As a first principle you must answer the set question and not another question that you had hoped for in the exam or essay.

❝ Discuss effective strategies for treating drug-using offenders. ❞

Directly relevant points

- Cognitive behavioural therapies have been shown to work well with addicted behaviours including drug addicts

Less relevant points

- Much drug crime is disorganised and acquisitive; and situational crime prevention may prevent it

- Replacement prescribing of heroin and methadone can prevent the need to engage in crime

- Drug users commit lots of crimes

- Such treatments can be effective, and many people believe £1 spent on treatment results in £3 less crime

- There can be risks involved in taking drugs

- Many people believe that for treatment to be effective it should be voluntristic rather than coercive

- Prison stops some people committing crime

- Drug Treatment and Testing Orders (DTTOs) and some forms of coercive treatment do seem to suggest, however, that they reduce drug use, and therefore related crime.

- Strain theory suggests drug use might be attempts to retreat from society.

Although some of the points listed in the second column may be relevant, they may be less relevant. It is part of your task to make sure that you answer the question. You can use some less relevant information, but the directly relevant points above are directly relevant because they meet the requirements of the question.

Common pitfall: Students sometimes have a wealth of information ready to draw upon, which they will write down, even when it is of little relevance to the subject under discussion. This very often results in an 'all I know about' essay that lacks structure. Try to be pertinent to the point under discussion and resist the temptation to use information that is not directly relevant to the question.

Missing your question

I have made this point before, but it is worth re-stating – the habit of 'question spotting' is always a risky game to play, and you should never take for granted what may appear on an exam. However, the reality is often that the question a student might be looking for is there, but they have not seen it. Some expect the question to be couched in certain words and cannot find these when they scanned over the questions in blind panic. Therefore, the simple lesson is always read over the questions carefully, slowly and thoughtfully. This practice is time well spent. Also bear in mind that terms in criminology may vary. You will probably fail your exam if you revise 'right realist' criminology without knowing the exam question might ask you to critique 'neo-conservative' criminology. On such simple misunderstandings students fail exams.

Write it down

If you write down the question you have chosen to address, and perhaps quietly articulate it with your lips, you are more likely to process fully its true meaning and intent. Think of how easy it is to misunderstand a question that has been put to you verbally because you have misinterpreted the tone or emphasis.

Pursue a critical approach

In degree courses you are usually expected to write critically rather than merely descriptively, although it may be necessary to use some minimal descriptive substance as the raw material for your debate.

Given that most questions will require some form of critical evaluation of the evidence or theory, you should prepare to address the issues one by one from both standpoints. What you should not do is digress into a tangent about the irrelevant or abstract information (often weak students will draw upon 'I think that ...' or 'common sense' arguments more suited to tabloid newspapers).

Analyse the parts

In an effective sports team the end product is always greater than the sum of the parts. Similarly, a good essay cannot be constructed without reference to the parts. Furthermore, the parts will arise as you break down the question into the components it suggests to you. Although the breaking down of a question into components is not sufficient for an excellent essay, it is a necessary starting point.

" Trace in a critical manner western society's changing attitudes to the corporal punishment of children. "

In this case you might want to consider the role of governments, the church, schools, parents and the media. However, you will need to have some reference points to the past as you are asked to address the issue of change. There would also be scope to look at where the strongest influences for change arise and where the strongest resistance comes from. You might argue that the changes have been dramatic or evolutionary, you may argue not. You might want to support your argument with reference to 'social theory', such as Norbert Elias' 'civilising process'.

Checklist: Ensuring that questions are understood before being fully addressed

✓ Read over the chosen question several times
✓ Write it down to ensure that it is clear
✓ Check that you have not omitted any important aspect or point of emphasis
✓ Ensure that you do not wrongly impose preconceived expectations on the question
✓ Break the question into parts (dismantle and rebuild).

Checklist: Write your own checklist on any additional points of guidance for exams that you have picked up from tutors or textbooks:

✓ ....
✓ ....
✓ ....
✓ ....
✓ ....

When asked to discuss

Students often ask how much of their own opinion they should include in an essay. In a discussion, when you raise one issue, another one can arise out of it. It is important that you recognise that your aim should be not just to identify and define all the parts that contribute, but also to show where they fit (or don't fit) into the overall picture.

Checklist: Features of a response to a 'discuss' question

✓ Contains a chain of issues that lead into each other in sequence
✓ Clear shape and direction is unfolded in the progression of the argument
✓ Underpinned by reference to findings and certainties
✓ Identification of issues where doubt remains
✓ Tone of argument may be tentative but should not be vague.

If a critique is requested

One example that might help clarify what is involved in a critique is the hotly debated topic of the physical punishment of children. It would be important in the interest of balance and fairness to present all sides and shades of the argument. You would then look at whether there is available evidence to support each argument, and you might introduce issues that have been coloured by prejudice, tradition, religion and legislation. It would be an aim to identify emotional arguments, arguments based on intuition and to get down to those arguments that really have solid evidence-based support. Finally you would want to flag up where the strongest evidence appears to lie, and you should also identify issues that appear to be inconclusive. It would be expected that you should, if possible, arrive at some conclusions.

If asked to compare and contrast

When asked to compare and contrast, you should be thinking in terms of similarities and differences. You should ask what the two issues share in common, and what features of each are distinct. Your preferred strategy for tackling this might be to work first through all the similarities and then through all the contrasts (or vice versa). Or, on the other hand, to work through a similarity and a contrast, followed by another similarity and contrast etc.

"Compare and contrast right and left realism."

Similarities

- Both believed crime rates had risen from the late 1970s
- Both thought crime to be damaging, and had real negative effects on victims and communities
- Both believed there is the need for academic criminologists to produce research that helps to develop realistic policy that will feed into practices that counter the 'crime problem'
- Both are more concerned with the 'crimes of the street' than 'crimes of the elites'
- Both regard the community as a part of the solution to crime problems.

Contrasts

- They are informed by different political ideology
- Difference in terms of perceptions about 'solutions to crime'
- Difference of opinion as to whether crime is freely chosen
- Divided in terms of the notion that the state should withdraw from delivery of services.

Whenever evaluation is requested

A worked example of evaluation

"Imagine that you are a researcher asked to investigate the extent of the effect of a police pilot initiative to reduce the rate of burglary in three roads, by promoting property marking, and offering residents security advice on one inner city estate where the crime rate is high. How would you go about this?"

As part of your task you might want to review past features (retrospectively), such as, what was the previous extent of burglary. You might want to outline present features (perspective) such as the resident's views of the scheme, and envisage positive future changes (prospective). Indeed, in being asked to do an evaluation you are being asked, to an extent, to select your focus (and there may be an extensive list of things that could be relevant).

This illustration may provoke you to think about how you might approach a question. If it does it has served its purpose, because generally evaluating something requires you to ask searching questions. If you encounter a question that asks you to evaluate some theory in criminology, you can draw upon the criteria for evaluating theory. If you are asked to evaluate a scheme or project you might find the following questions stimulating:

- How can I find out if this scheme/project has had an effect?
- Has the scheme/project demonstrated any effect?
- Does the scheme/project have a supportive theoretical/evidence base?
- Is this evidence robust?
- Where does it come from?
- How was it generated?
- Are there questionable elements that have been or should be challenged?
- Does more recent evidence point to a need for modification?
- Are there aspect(s) that can be improved?
- Have there been any unforeseen 'side-effects'? (For example, in relation to the above example, have the burglars just moved to new streets?)
- Could it be strengthened through being merged with other theories/concept?

Checklist: Write your own checklist on what you remember or understand about each of the following: 'Discuss', 'Compare and Contrast', 'Evaluate' and 'Critique' (just a key word or two for each). If you find this difficult then you should read this chapter again and then try once more.

✓ ....

✓ ....

✓ ....

✓ ....

It should be noted that the words presented in the above examples might not always be the exact words that will appear on your exam script, for example, you might find 'analyse', 'outline' or 'investigate' etc. The best advice is to check over your past exam papers and familiarise yourself with the words that are most recurrent.

In summary, this chapter has been designed to give you reference points to measure where you are at in your studies, and to help you map out the way ahead in manageable increments. It should now be clear that learning should not merely be a mechanical exercise, such as just memorising and reproducing study material. Quality learning also involves making connections between ideas, thinking at a deeper level by attempting to understand your material and developing a critical approach to learning. However, this cannot be achieved without the discipline of preparation for lectures, seminars and exams, or without learning to structure your material (headings and subheadings) and to set each unit of learning within its overall context in your subject and programme. An important device in learning is to develop the ability to ask questions (whether written, spoken or silent). Another useful device in learning is to illustrate your material and use examples that will help make your study fun, memorable and vivid. It is useful to set problems for yourself that will allow you to think through solutions and therefore enhance the quality of your learning.

On the one hand there are the necessary disciplined procedures such as preparation before each learning activity and consolidation afterwards. It is also vital to keep your subject materials in organised folders so that you can add/extract/replace materials when you need to. On the other hand there is the need to develop personality qualities such as feeding your confidence, fuelling your motivation and turning stress responses to your advantage. This chapter has presented strategies to guide you through finding the balance between these organised and dynamic aspects of academic life.

Your aim should be to become an 'all round student' who engages in and benefits from all the learning activities available to you (lectures, seminars, tutorials, computing, labs, discussions, library work etc.), and to develop all the academic and personal skills that will put you in the driving seat to academic achievement. It will be motivating and confidence building for you, if you can recognise the value of these qualities, both across your academic programme and beyond graduation to the world of work. They will also serve you well in your continued commitment to life-long learning.

part four

additional resources

glossary of key terms and criminologists

Abolitionism

A term that is used to describe the theoretical opposition to imprisonment.

Actuarial/actuarialism

A term that is used to describe risk assessment and calculation techniques associated with correctional policies and treatments.

Aetiology

The study of the causes or origins of behaviour. Positivistic approaches in criminology are characterised by their interest in determining the aetiology of criminal acts, for example, 'the work of Lombroso was concerned with the aetiology of criminality...'

Adler, Freda

Notable for her theory, in her work *Sisters in Crime* (1975), that women's liberation had resulted in increased instances of female crime.

Administrative

criminology

Criminology that is linked to the political administration and emerged in Britain circa 1980. It is associated with rational choice perspectives and situational crime prevention.

Anomie

Refers to a social condition involving individuals and society (especially at periods of transition), when norms governing social interaction are limited or cease to exist.

Atavism

A term used by Lombroso; who suggested that while most individuals evolve, some devolve, becoming primitive or 'atavistic'. These evolutionary 'throwbacks' are 'born criminals' – the most violent criminals in society.

Beccaria, Cesare

A founder of the classical school of criminological thought in On *Crimes and Punishments* (1764) [1963].

Becker, Howard

A prominent sociologist, Becker's work *Outsiders: Studies in the sociology of deviance* (1963) and *The Other Side* (1964) are significant works in the interactionist/new deviancy tradition, that developed the concept of 'labelling theory'.

Bentham, Jeremy

Founder of the concept of utilitarianism, designer of the Panoptican Prison, and is associated with what is termed 'classical criminology'.

Bottoms, Sir Anthony

An eminent Professor of Criminology who has written extensively on the subjects of legal process, criminal justice and imprisonment.

Carceral

A term used by Foucault (1977) to describe the role of the state as it moved to using imprisonment, and its concern with disciplining and monitoring its subjects.

Carlen, Pat

A leading feminist who has written extensively on issues relating to women, crime and imprisonment.

Christie, Nils

A Professor of Criminology at the University of Oslo, who has written extensively on punishment and imprisonment, dangerous offenders, and criminal justice in Norway. He is also associated with the ideas of *Crime Control as Industry* where he argues crime control is potentially as dangerous as crime itself (1994) and *The Ideal Victim* (1986).

Classicism

A term used to describe the early criminology, particularly the works of Cesare Beccaria, and the suggestion that crime is a product of freewill.

Cohen, Stan

Made numerous contributions to sociology and criminology on a range of issues relating to criminology and criminal justice, perhaps most notably *Folk Devils and Moral Panics* (1972).

Control theory

A theory associated predominantly with Travis Hirschi that suggests that weakened social bonds and a lack of social attachment can contribute to delinquency.

Corporate crime

A term that is used to refer to breaches of criminal or civil law by organisations, whether by acts or omissions, and often reflects the values and priorities of the corporation.

Crime

Not fixed or static but changes. The term crime at its most basic describes an activity which breaches criminal law; however what activity should constitute crime is fiercely contested (see Chapter 1.5).

Criminology

A term that is used to describe an eclectic range of contributions that consider in the most part the creation of law, criminal conduct and its regulation and control (law-making, law-breaking and law enforcement) but also bolstered by discussion of 'deviant' and 'delinquent' behaviour.

Critical

A term used in criminology to describe criminological works that draw upon the conflict tradition in criminology, for example, the work of Ian Taylor (1999).

Currie, Elliot

Associated with left realist criminology in America. His works include *Confronting Crime* (1985) and *Crime and Punishment in America* (1998).

Cybercrime

A term used to describe criminal and deviant activities that involve the use of new technology, most notably the internet and the world-wide web.

Dark figure

A term that is used to describe and refer to specific criminal acts that are not recorded in official crime statistics, or are not repre-sented/significantly under recorded (this is also sometimes refered to as invisible or hidden crime).

Delinquency

A term which is used to refer to a range of youthful misbehaviour.

Determinism

There is no single definition of determinism, but in essence it is used in criminology to counter the philosophy of freewill, suggesting that indi-viduals may be propelled towards a criminality by factors over which they have little, if any, control.

Deterrence

A strategy of punishment associated with clas-sicism. Deterrence can either be specific where it aims to punish the individual so that they won't commit a crime again, or general, punish-ing an individual to set an example to society, so that others will not commit the same crime.

Deviance

Behaviour that is disapproved of, marginal, not common or accepted, but is not in the strict sense criminal.

Deviancy amplification   A concept associated with Leslie Wilkins that describes the way that attempts to control deviant acts by the state and its agents actually have the reverse effect and increase deviance.

Differential association   A concept associated with Sutherland that suggests criminal skills are learnt and transferred in social interaction.

Differential opportunity   A theory used by Cloward and Ohlin (1960) to describe juvenile delinquency; essentially an amalgamation of differential association and strain theories.

Drift   A concept associated with subculture studies of delinquency and David Matza (1964). It describes the way that young people literally 'drift' in and out of criminality.

Epistemology   Means 'theories of knowledge' and describes beliefs about the nature of the world and how we should generate knowledge.

Ethnography   A research method drawn from anthropology and the study of people and groups in their natural setting. Typically this involves the researcher spending prolonged periods of time in order to gather data about their day-to-day activities. As a research method it is associated with the Chicago School of Sociology.

Farrington, David   An eminent professor of Criminology, in particular his expertise is criminal psychology and delinquency. He has been hugely influential in developing and mapping factors likely to lead to delinquency and in developing the understanding of criminal careers.

Felson, Marcus

A leading administrative criminologist whose most notable work is *Crime and Everyday Life* (2002).

Feminism

A term used to describe perspectives that share a concern with the inequality of women and discrimination against them, by assuming that theories about male behaviour are applicable to the experiences of women.

Ferrell, Jeff

One of the driving forces behind more recent 'cultural' criminology, and has produced ethnic research on youth subculture and resistance.

Folk devil

A term that is used to describe those who are the subjects of moral panics and popular myths.

Foucault, Michael

Mmost noted for introducing the notion of The 'carceral society' in his book *Discipline and Punish* (1977) but also provided a great many philosophical writings that have proved influential upon criminology.

Freewill

The notion that people actively chose their behaviour, and are not determined by factors beyond their control. It is the theoretical basis of works in the classical tradition in criminology, but also informs right realist and administrative criminology.

Garland, David

A Professor of Criminology at New York University who has published extensive studies on criminal sanctions, the theory and practice of incarceration and law and modern society.

Goffman, Erving

A sociologist who is notable for his contributions *Asylums* (1961) and *Stigma* (1963) in the interactionist tradition which are significant to issues of imprisonment and deviance.

Governmentality

A term that is used to describe an approach in criminology that focuses upon the way in which the state government is both planned and operates technically by responding to problems that are to be governed.

Hegemony

A term used by sociologists to describe how the domination of one class over others is achieved. In criminology it is a term that is often used by masculinity theorists.

Hidden crime

Refers to crimes, or categories of crime that are not found in official crime statistics (see **Dark figure**).

Hirschi, Travis

An American criminologist associated with control and social bond theory, arguing that the presence of social bonds and controls make individuals less likely to be deviant or criminal.

Hobbs, Dick

Has written extensively on the subject of ethnography in criminology, serious, professional organised and violent crime and qualitative research on criminals.

Hood, Roger

Has written on a range of subjects, including penal policy, the history of the English criminal law, perspectives on the death penalty and race and sentencing in the courts.

Incapacitation

Refers to a theory of punishment that is concerned with limiting the offender's ability to commit further crime.

Katz, Jack

Regarded as having been a leading influence upon criminology's most recent 'cultural' theories. Katz's *Seductions of Crime* (1988) was the first criminological work to examine the emotion that underpins much criminality.

Lemert Edwin

A sociologist/anthropologist who built upon interaction criminology, new deviancy and labelling theories to develop the concepts of primary and secondary deviation and the way in which evil can be used in the study of deviance (see *The Trouble with Evil,* 1997).

Lombroso, Cesare

Regarded by some as the father of modern criminology, Lombroso was a founder of the Italian positivistic school of criminology, and is associated with mapping atavism, and the notion that criminals could be born.

Mathiesen, Thomas

Has written extensively on the issue of imprisonment and is particularly associated with prison 'abolitionism'.

Matza, David

Contributed to subculture and delinquency studies, and developed criminological theories in relation to *Techniques of Neutralisation* (with Gresham Sykes, 1957) and *Delinquency and Drift* (1964).

Merton, Robert

A prominent functionalist criminologist who is associated with 'strain theory'.

Moral panic

A term coined by Cohen to describe disproportionate reaction to a perceived threat to society's values, particularly involving media representation and exaggeration which creates a public appetite for increased regulation and social control.

Murray, Charles

A prominent right realist, Murray is associated with the notion of the 'underclass' and the belief that 'prison works'.

Organisational crime

A term that refers to corporate crime or criminality involving supposedly legitimate organisations.

Organised crime

A term used to describe serious and often collective criminality that is difficult to control, but presents specific threat to the autonomy and power of the state.

Panopticon

Stemming from Jeremy Bentham's prison design, the term refers to a condition of observational visibility, inspection (and therefore control) that has spread into society more generally concerned with regulation; the 'carceral' society (Foucault, 1977).

Positivism

A theoretical approach that emerged during the early nineteenth century which argued that it was possible to study society and social phenomena (such as crime) using methods derived from the natural sciences. In criminology it can be biological, psychological and sociological in orientation.

Qualitative methods

Describes social research inquiry associated with statistics, probability and data, and often, though not always, linked with positivistic research methods.

Quantitative methods

Involves social research inquiry concerned with human interaction and contact (often based upon interview and observation) rather than measurable data.

Quetelet, Adolphe   A 'moral statistician' and one of the first to propose the detailed study of social statistics including criminal statistics.

Realism   Describes an approach to criminology that emerged during the late 1970s and tends to be affiliated to either the political right or left, but regardless, shares a concern with rising crime rates and the damage that crime does, and argues that criminologists should exert influence upon policy by generating useful research.

Recidivism   A term used in criminology to describe re-offending, for example, 'the recidivist offender...'

Reiner, Robert   A criminologist who writes extensively on police and policing, police culture and issues relating to the media and crime.

Smart, Carol   A leading feminist who has written on a wide range of issues in relation to women and the criminal justice system.

Social disorganisation   A concept associated with the Chicago School of Criminology which suggests that community breakdown and lack of attachment to society's institutions can result in criminality.

Social learning   A psychological and sociological approach that suggests that people's behaviour is influenced by the dual relationship between person and environment.

Social theory   A term that is used to describe the sometimes complicated and theoretical ideas that are used to describe social patterns and social structures.

Strain	A criminological theory associated with Robert Merton which suggests that lack of access to legitimate opportunities can result in criminality.
Subculture	Associated with attempts to study juvenile delinquency, and the way in which the values and attitudes of some young people differ from those of 'normal' society.
Sutherland, Edwin Harding	Produced numerous publications and is one of the most prominent and influential criminologists in the subject's history. He is associated with debate on 'white collar crime', and professional criminality, and developed the theory of 'differential association'.
Taylor, Ian	A criminologist in the critical tradition who is most noted for his works *The New Criminology* (with Paul Walton and Jock Young, 1973) and *Crime in Context* (1999) His last book before his death in 2001.
Young, Jock	One of Britain's leading criminologists who has written a vast amount on the subject of criminology in the interactionist tradition in *The Drugtakers* (1971) and as a conflict/critical criminologist in The *New Criminology* (with Ian Taylor and Paul Walton, 1973). He also introduced the notion of left realist criminology in *What is to be Done about Law and Order?* (with John Lea, 1984) and most recently, has turned to 'cultural criminology'.
White collar crime	A term that is used to signify crimes that are committed by 'respectable people' in the course of their occupation.

Wilson, David

A former prison Governor who writes extensively on prisons and imprisonment, but is also one of the criminologists you are most likely to encounter on television documentaries and news programmes. He categorises himself as a left idealist criminologist, and is outspoken on a range of matters relating to criminal justice policy.

Wilson, James Q.

Perhaps the most prominent right realist criminologist he has contributed extensively to criminology on matters such as psychology and crime (with Richard Herrnstein, 1984) and was instrumental in bringing realist criminology to the fore with *Thinking about Crime* (1975). He has also developed the theory of 'broken windows' (with George Kelling, 1982).

bibliography

Adler, F. (1975) *Sisters in Crime*, New York: McGraw Hill.

Agnew, R. (1992) 'Foundations for a general strain theory of crime and delinquency', *Criminology*, 30 (1): 47–87.

Ainswortyh, P. (2001) *Offender Profiling and Crime Analysis*, Cullompton: Willan.

Amir, M. (1971) *Patterns of Forcible Rape*, Chicago: University of Chicago Press.

Beccaria, C. ((1764) [1963]) *On Crimes and Punishments*, New York: Bobbs-Merill.

Becker, H. (1963) *Outsiders: Studies in the Sociology of Deviance*, New York: Free Press.

Becker, H. (1964) *The Other Side: Perspective on Deviance,* New York: Free Press.

Biernie, P. (1994) *The Origins and Growth of Criminology*, Aldershot: Dartmouth.

Blackburn, R. (1993) *The Psychology of Criminal Conduct*, Chester: Wiley.

Blackstone, W. (1756 [1856]) *A Trestie on the Laws of England*, London: W.G. Benning & Co.

Bonger, W. (1916) *Criminality and Economic Conditions*, Boston: Little Brown.

Bonger, W. (1936) *An Introduction to Criminology*, London: Methuen and Co.

Bottoms, AE. (1980) 'An Introduction to "The Coming Crisis"' in AE. Bottoms and RH. Preston (eds) *The Coming Penal Crisis: A Criminological and Theological Explanation*, Edinburgh: Scottish Academy.

Bowling, B. and Phillips, C. (2002) *Race, Crime and Justice,* London: Longman.

Box, S. (1983) *Power, Crime and Mystification*, London: Tavistock.

Braithwaite, J. (1989) *Crime, Shame and Reintergration*, Cambridge: Cambridge University Press.

Braithwaite, J. (2001) *Restorative Justice and Responsive Regulation,* Oxford: Oxford University Press.

Campbell, B. (1993) *Goliath: Britain's Dangerous Places*, London: Methuen.

Carlen, P. (1983) *Women's Imprisonment*, London: Routledge and Keegan Paul.

Carlson, WG. (1981) *The Other Price of British Oil*, London: Martin Robertson.

Cavidino, M. and Dignan, J. (2002) *The Penal System* (2nd edn.), London: Sage.

Chambliss, W. (1978) *On the Take: From Petty Crooks to Presidents*, Bloomington: Indiana University Press.

Chapman, J. (1980) *Economic Realities and the Female Offender*, Lexington Books: Mass.

Christie, N. (1986) 'The Ideal Victim' in EA. Fattah (ed.) *From Crime Policy to Victim Policy*, London: Macmillan.

Christie, N. (1994) *Crime Control as Industry*, London: Routledge.

Clarke, RV. (1997) *Situational Crime Prevention: Successful case studies* (2nd edn.), New York: Harrow and Heston.

Cloward, R. and Ohlin, L. (1960) *Delinquency and Opportunity: A Theory of Delinquent Gangs*, New York: Free Press.

Cohen, A. (1955) *Delinquent Boys: The Culture of the Gang*, New York: Free Press.

Cohen, S. (1972) *Folk Devils and Moral Panics,* London: McGibbon and Kee.

Coleman, C. and Moynihan, J. (1996) *Understanding Crime Data: Haunted by the Dark Figure*, Buckingham: Open University Press.

Coleman, C. and Norris, C. (2000) *Introducing Criminology*, Cullompton: Willan.

Connell, RW. (1987) *Gender and Power*, Cambridge: Polity Press.

Connell, RW. (1995) *Masculinities*, Cambridge: Polity Press.

Cornish, D. and Clarke, RV. (eds) (1996) *The Reasoning Criminal: Rational Choice Perspectives on Offending*, New York: Springer-Verlag.

Croall, H. (2001) *Understanding White Collar Crime,* Buckingham: Open University Press.

Crow, I. (2001) *The Treatment and Rehabilitation of Offenders*, London: Sage.

Cullen, E. and Newell, T. (1999) *Murderers and Life Imprisonment*, Winchester: Waterside Press.

Currie, E. (1985) *Confronting Crime: An American Challenge,* New York: Pantheon Books.

Currie, E. (1998) *Crime and Punishment in America*, New York: Metropolitan Books.

Daly, K. and Maher, L. (1998) *Criminology at the Crossroads: Feminist Readings on Crime and Justice*, Oxford: Oxford University Press.

Darwin, C. (1885) *The Descent of Man*, London: John Murray.

Devlin, A. and Turney, B. (1999) *Going Straight*, Winchester: Waterside Press.

Downes, D. (1966) *The Delinquent Solution*, London: Routledge.

Downes, D. and Morgan, R. (1997) 'Dumping the "Hostages to fortune" The Politics of Law and Order in Post-War Britain' in M. Maguire, R. Morgan and R. Reiner (1997) *The Oxford Handbook of Criminology* (2nd edn.), Oxford: Oxford University Press.

Downes, D. and Rock, P. (1998) *Understanding Deviance* (3rd edn.) Oxford: Oxford University Press.

Durkheim, E. (1895 [1952]) *Suicide: A Study in Sociology*, London: Routledge and Keegan Paul.

Ellias, N. (1994) *The Civilising Process*, Oxford: Blackwell.

Eysenck, H. ((1964) [1977]) *Crime and Personality*, London: Routledge and Keegan Paul.

Felson, M. (2002) *Crime and Everyday Life*, (3rd edn.) Thousand Oaks, CA: Sage Publications.

Felson, M. and Clarke, RV. (1998) *Opportunity Makes the Thief: Practical Theory for Crime Prevention*, Aldershot: Ashgate.

Ferrell, J. (2001) 'Cultural Criminology' in E. McLaughlin and J. Muncie (eds) *The Sage Dictionary of Criminology* (2nd edn.), London: Sage.

Ferrell, J. and Saunders, C. (eds) (1995) *Cultural Criminology*, Boston: Northeastern University Press.

Ferrell, J., Hayward, K., Morrison, W. and Presdee, M. (2004) (eds) *Cultural Criminology Unleashed*, London: GlassHouse.

Ferri, E. (1895) *Criminal Sociology*, London: T. Fisher Unwin.

Foucault, M. (1977) *Discipline and Punish*, Harmondsworth: Penguin.

Garland D. (2001a) *The culture of Control: Crime and Social Order in Contemporary Society*, Oxford: Oxford University Press.

Garland, D. (ed.) (2001b) *Mass Imprisonment: Social Causes and Consequences*, London: Sage.

Garland, D. (2002) 'Of Crimes and Criminals: The Development of Criminology in Britain', in M. Maguire, R. Morgan and R. Reiner (eds) *The Oxford Handbook of Criminology* (3rd edn.), Oxford: Oxford University Press.

Goffman, E. (1961) *Asylums*, New York: Anchor.

Goffman, E. (1963) *Stigma*, New York: Simon and Schuster.

Goode, E. and Ben-Yehuda, N. (1994) *Moral Panics: The Social Construction of Deviance*, Oxford: Blackwell.

Gottfredson, M. and Hirschi, T. (1990) *A General Theory of Crime*, Stanford: Stanford University Press.

Hall, S. and Jefferson, T. (1976) *Resistance Through Rituals*, London: Routledge.

Hall, S., Critcher, C., Jefferson, T., Clarke, J. and Roberts, B. (1978) *Policing the Crisis: Mugging, The State and Law and Order*, London: MacMillan Press.

Hamner, J. and Saunders, S. (1984) *Well Founded Fear: Community study of violence to women*, London: Harper Collins.

Hare, R. (1993) *Without Conscience*, London: The Guilford Press.

Hickey, E. (1997) *Serial Murders and their Victims*, Belmont: Wandsworth.

Hirschi, T. (1969) *Causes of Delinquency*, California: University of California Press.

HMIP (2004) *Juveniles in Custody*, London: HMSO.

Holmes, RM. and DeBurger (1988) *Serial Murder*, Newbury Park: Sage.

Holmes, RM. and Holmes, ST. (1998) *Serial Murder*, London: Sage.

James, E. (2003) *A Life Inside*, London: Guardian Books.

Jewkes, Y. (2004) *Media and Crime*, London: Sage.

Jewkes, Y. and Leatherby, G. (2002) *Criminology: A reader*, London: Sage.

Jones, T. Mclean, and Young, J. (1986) *The Islington Crime Survey*, Aldershot: Gower.

Jupp, V. (1989) *Methods of Criminological Research*, London: Unwin Hyman.

Jupp, V., Davies, P. and Francis, P. (2000) *Doing Criminological Research*, London: Sage.

Katz, J. (1988) *The Seductions of Crime: Moral and Sensual Attractions in Doing Evil*, New York: Basic Books.

Kiger, K. (1990) 'The Darker Figure of Crime: The serial Murder Enigma' in S. Egger (ed.) *Serial Murder: an Elusive Phenomenon*, New York: Praeger.

Kinsey, R. (1985) *Merseyside Crime and Police Survey Final Report*, Centre for Criminology, University of Edinburgh.

Lange, J. (1931) *Crime as Destiny*, London: Allen and Unwin.

Lea, J. and Young, J. (1984) *What is to be Done about Law and Order?*, Harmondsworth: Penguin.

Lemert, E. (1972) *Human Deviance, Social Problems, Social Control*, NJ: Prentice Hall.

Lemert, E. (1997) *The Trouble with Evil: Social Control at the Edge of Morality*, Albany: SUNY Press.

Leyton, E. (1989) *Hunting Humans: The Rise of the Modern Multiple Murderer* Harmondsworth: Penguin.

Lombroso, C. (1876) *L'Uomo Delinquente*, Milan: Hoepli.

Lombroso, C. and Ferrero, W. (1895) *The Female Offender*, London: Fisher Unwin.

Maguire, M. (2002) 'Crime Statistics: The "data explosion" and its implications' in M. McGuire, R. Morgan and R. Reiner (eds) *The Oxford Handbook of Criminology*, Oxford: Oxford University Press.

Maguire, M., Morgan, R. and Reiner, R. (1997) *The Oxford Handbook of Criminology* (2nd edn.) Oxford: Oxford University Press.

Marshall, T. (1999) *Restorative Justice*, London: Home Office.

Martinson, R. (1974) 'What Works?: Questions and Answers about Prison Reform' in *The Public Interest* 35: 22–54.

Matza, D. (1964) *Delinquency and Drift*, London: Wiley.

Matza, D. (1969) *Becoming Deviant*, Englewood Ciffs, NJ: Prentice Hall.

Mawby, R. and Walklate, S. (1994) *Critical Victimology*, London: Sage.

May, T. (2001) *Social Research: Issues, Methods and Processes*, Buckingham: Open University Press.

Mayhew, P. (2000) 'Researching the State of Crime: Local, National and International Victim Surveys', in RD. King and E. Wincup (eds) *Doing Research on Crime and Justice*, Oxford: Oxford University Press.

Mays, J. (1954) *Growing Up in the City*, Liverpool: Liverpool University Press.

McGuire, J. and Priestley, P. (1995) 'Reviewing What Works' in J. McGuire (ed.) *What Works*, Chichester: John Wiley.

McIlroy, D. (2003) *Studying at University: How to be a Successful Student*, London: Sage.

McLaughlin, E. and Muncie, J. (2001) *The Sage Dictionary of Criminology*, London: Sage.

McLaughlin, E., Muncie, J. and Hughes, G. (2003) *Criminological Perspectives. Essential Readings*, London: Sage.

McRobbie, A. and Thornton, S. (1995) 'Rethinking "moral panic" for multi-mediated social worlds' *British Journal of Sociology* 46 (4): 559–74.

Merton, R. (1938) 'Social Structure and Anomie', *American Sociological Review* 3: 672–82.

Merton, R. (1968) *Social Theory and Social Structure*, New York: Free Press.

Messerschmidt, J. (1993) *Masculinity and Crime,* Boston: Rowman and Littlefield.

Michael, J. and Alder, M. (1933) *Crime, Law and Social Science*, New York: Harcourt Brace Jovanovich.

Michalowski, R. (1985) *Order, Law and Crime,* New York: Random House.

Morrison, B. (1998) *As If*, London: Granta Books.

Muncie, J. (1999) *Youth and Crime*, London: Sage.

Muncie, J. (2000) 'Decriminalising Criminology' in G. Lewis, G. Gewirtz and J. Clarke (eds) *Rethinking Social Policy*, London: Sage.

Muncie, J. and McLaughlin, E. (2001) *The Problem of Crime*, London: Sage.

Muncie, J. and Wilson, D. (eds) (2004) *The Student Handbook of Criminal Justice and Criminology*, London: Cavandish.

Murray, C. (1984) *Losing Ground*, New York: Basic Books.

Murray, C. (1990) *The Emerging Underclass*, London: Institute for Economic Affairs.

Murray, C. (1994) *Underclass: The Crisis Deepens,* London: Institute for Economic Affairs.

Naylor, RT. (1997) 'Mafias, myths and markets', *Transnational Organised Crime* 3 (3): 15–30.

Newburn, T. (2002) *Young People, Crime and Youth Justice*, Devon: Willan.

Newburn, T. and Stanko, E. (1995) *Just Boys Doing Business*, London: Routledge.

Parenti, C. (1999) *Lockdown America: Police and Prisons in the Age of Crisis,* London: Verso.

Park, R., Burgess, EW. and McKenzie, RD. (1925) *The City*, Chicago: University of Chicago Press.

Pearson, G. (1975) *The Deviant Imagination*, London: Macmillan.

Pearson, G. (1983) *Hooligan: A History of Respectable Fears*, London: MacMillan.

Pepinsky, H. and Quinney, R. (1991) (eds) *Criminology as Peacemaking*, Bloomington: Indiana University Press.

Pollack, O. (1950) *The Criminality of Women*, New York: AS Barnes.

Punch, M. (1996) *Dirty Business: Exploring corporate misconduct*, London: Sage.

Quetelet, A. (1842) *A Treatise on Man*, Edinburgh: Chambers.

Quinney, R. (1970) *The Social Reality of Crime*, Boston MA: Little Brown.

Quinney, R. (1974) *Critique of Legal Order: Crime Control in Capitalist Society*, Boston, MA: Little Brown.

Quinney, R. (1980 [1977]) *Class, State and Crime: On the Theory and Practice of Criminal Justice*, New York: McKay.

Quinney, R. (1993) 'A Life of Crime: Criminology and Public policy as Peacemaking', *Journal of Crime and Justice* 16: 3–9.

Radzinowicz, L. (1999) *Adventures in Criminology*, London: Routledge.

Roche, D. (2003) *Accountability in Restorative Justice*, Oxford: Oxford University Press.

Schur, E. (1965) *Crimes Without Victims*, Englewood Cliffs, NJ: Prentice Hall.

Schur, E. (1973) *Radical Non-intervention*, Englewood Cliffs NJ: Prentice Hall.

Schwendinger, H. and Schwendinger, J. (1970) 'Defenders of Order or Guardians of Human Rights', *Issues in Criminology* 5: 123–57.

Sellin, T. (1938) *Culture, Conflict and Crime*, New York: Social Research Council.

Shaw, CR. (1930) *The Jack Roller: a delinquent boy's own story*, Chicago: University of Chicago press.

Shaw, C. and McKay, H. (1942) *Juvenille Delinquency in Urban Areas*, Chicago: University of Chicago Press.

Silverman, J. and Wilson, D. (2002) *Innocence Betrayed*, Cambridge: Polity Press.

Sim, J. (2004) 'Thinking about imprisonment' in J. Muncie and D. Wilson (eds) *Student Handbook of Criminal Justice and Criminology*, London: Cavendish.

Slapper, G. and Tombs, S. (1999) *Corporate Crime*, London: Longman.

Smart, C. (1976) *Women, Crime and Criminology*, London: Routledge and Keegan Paul.

Smart, C. (1979) 'The New Female Criminal: Reality or Myth?', *British Journal of Criminology*, 19: 50–59.

Smith, P. and Natalier, K. (2004) *Understanding Criminal Justice: Sociological Perspectives*, London: Sage.

Smith, R. (2003) *Youth Justice: Ideas, Policy, Practice*, Cullompton: Willan.

Stanko, E. (1998) *Counting the Costs*. London: Crime Concern.

Sutherland, EH. (1937) *The Professional Thief*, Chicago: University of Chicago Press.

Sutherland, EH. (1939) *Principles of Criminology*, Philadelphia: Lippincott.

Sutherland, EH. (1945) 'Is White Collar Crime Crime?', *American Sociological Review* 10 (2): 132–39.

Sutherland, EH. (1949) *White Collar Crime*, New York: Dryden.

Sutherland, EH. and Cressey, D. (1978) *Criminology* (10th edn.), Philidelphia: Lippincott.

Sykes, G. and Matza, D. (1957) 'Techniques of Neutralisation: A Theory of Delinquency', *American Sociological Review* 22: 664.

Tappan, P. (1947) 'Who is the Criminal?', *American Sociological Review* 12: 96–102.

Taylor, I. (1999) *Crime in Context*, Cambridge: Polity Press.

Taylor, I., Walton, P. and Young, J. (1973) *The New Criminology*, London: Routledge and Keegan Paul.

Taylor, I., Walton, P. and Young, J. (1975) *Critical Criminology*, London: Routledge and Keegan Paul.

Tennenbaum, F. (1938) *Crime and the Community*, New York: Ginn and Co.

Thrasher, F. (1927) *The Gang*, Chicago: University of Chicago Press.

Vold, G. (1958) *Theoretical Criminology*, New York: Oxford University Press.

Von Hentig, H. (1948) *The Criminal and his Victim*, New Haven: Yale University Press.

Waddington, PAJ. (1986) 'Mugging as a moral panic: a question of Proportion', *British Journal of Sociology*, 32(2): pp. 245–59.

Walklate, S. (2004) *Gender, Crime and Criminal Justice,* Devon: Willan.

Weisburd, D., Wheeler, S., Waring, E. and Bode, N. (1991) *Crimes of the Middle Classes: White Collar Offenders in the Federal Courts*, New Haven: Yale University Press.

Wilkins, L. (1964) *Social Deviancy*, London: Tavistock.

Williams, K. (2004) *Criminology* (5th edn.), Oxford: Oxford University Press.

Wilson, D. and Ashton, J. (2001) *What Everyone in Britain Should Know about Crime and Punishment* (2nd edn.), Oxford: Oxford University Press.

Wilson, D. and O'Sullivan, S. (2004) *Images of Incarceration: Representations of Prison in Film and Television Drama,* Winchester: Waterside Press.

Wilson, JQ. (1975) *Thinking About Crime*, New York: Basic Books.

Wilson, JQ. and Herrnstein, R. (1985) *Crime and Human Nature*, New York: Simon and Schuster.

Wilson, JQ. and Kelling, G. (1982) 'Broken Windows' in E. McLaughlin, J. Muncie and G. Hughes (2003) *Criminological Perspectives. Essential Readings*, London: Sage.

Wood, M. (2005) 'The victimisation of young people: Findings from the Crime and Justice Survey 2003', *Home Office Research Findings* 246, London: HMSO.

Woolfgang, M. (1958) *Patterns in Criminal Homicide*, Philadelphia: University of Pennsylvania Press.

Wright, G. and Hill, J. (2004) 'Victims, Crime and Criminal Justice' in J. Muncie and D. Wilson (eds) *Student Handbook of Criminal Justice and Criminology*, London: Cavendish.

Young, J. (1971) *The Drugtakers*, London: Paladin.

Young, J. (1999) *The Exclusive Society*, London: Sage.

Young, J. (2003) 'Merton with Energy, Katz with Structure', *Theoretical Criminology* 7 (3): 389–414.

index

abolitionism 100, 170
access 31
acronyms 153
actuarialism 170
Adler, Freda 91–2, 170
Adler, M. 8
administrative criminology 60–1, 170
aetiology 170
age, running themes 15
Agnew, Robert 48
agreement bonds 53
Alpha oil rig explosion 111
America, youth crime research 86–7
Amir, M. 119
anomie theories 48, 170
    criticisms 50–1
anonymity 30
ANS *see* autonomic nervous system
anthropometry 36
application of theory
    evaluating 131–2
    running themes 15
atavism 36, 170
attachment bonds 53
autonomic nervous system (ANS)
    156–7, 161

balanced essay writing 142–3
BCS *see* British Crime Survey
Beccaria, Cesare 16, 19–21, 171
Becker, Howard 11, 53–4, 171
Ben-Yehuda, N. 81–2
Bentham, Jeremy 17, 19, 171, 178
biological criminology 36–8
    cultural myths 37, 95
    female criminality 94–5
    influence and importance 40–1
Blackstone, William 19
bonds to society 52–3
boot-leggers 113
'born criminals' 36, 41, 170

bottom up clarity (essays) 148
Bottoms, Anthony 106, 171
Braithwaite, John 117–18, 123
Britain, youth crime research 86–7
British Crime Survey (BCS) 71–2
broadsheet newspapers 64, 73, 134
Bulger, James 78, 102
Burgess, Ernest W. 46

capital punishment *see* death penalty
capital system 18–19
capitalism 94
carceral punishment 104, 171
Carlen, Pat 92, 171
causation 26, 28
Chambliss, William 9–10
Chicago School of Sociology
    qualitative research methods 26–7
    social disorganisation theory 46–7
    youth crime research 86
children
    capital system 18
    criminal responsibility 78
    see also youth crime
Christie, Nils 171
citations (essay writing) 146, 160
clarity (essay writing) 148
class
    defining 51
    hegemony 176
    running themes 14
    status frustration 49
    strain theory 48–9
classical criminology 17–23, 172
    Beccaria 19–21
    capital system 18–19
    criticisms 21–2
    feudal system 18
    positivism contrast 35
    punishment 18–19, 20–1, 173
    spirituality 17–18

classical criminology *cont.*
  utilitarianism 19
  see also traditional criminology
clear-up rates 69–70
Cloward, Richard 50
Cohen, Albert 49
Cohen, Stan 76, 79–80, 172
combined research methods 27
commitment bonds 53
'compare and contrast'
    questions 165–6
conclusions (essays) 148
conflict theories 8–9, 44–5, 112
Connell, Robert 96
consensus theories 44
consent 30
contemporary criminology 55–66
context, learning 133
contributing to seminars 139
control
  deviancy amplification 79
  moral panics 80
  ruling class 20
control theory 52–3, 172
  white collar crime 111
Conwell, Chic 112
corporal punishment
  classical criminology 18
  essay tips 164
  historical phases of
    punishment 104
corporate crime 172
  victim surveys 72
costs, youth crime 86
covert research 31
crime
  definitions 6–7, 172
  perspectives 8–11
  statistics and data 66–75
criminal careers
  criticisms of concept 112
  predictors 86
  right realist approaches 57
criminalisation 84
criminology
  categorisation of theory 12
  definitions 5–6, 172
  origins 16–23
  research methods 24–33
  running themes 14–15

critical criminology 172
critical epistemology 28–9
critical mainstream accounts,
    prison crisis 106, 107–8
critical thinking 130–2, 152
critical victimology 122
critical writing 142, 163
'critique' questions 165
Croall, Hazel 111
cuffing 70
cultural criminology 27, 62–4
cultural myths 37, 95
cultural studies 63
cultural transmission 47
Currie, Elliot 172
cybercrime 173

'dark figure' of crime 69, 71–3, 173
data *see* statistics and data
death penalty 18, 20, 104
delinquency 173
  control theory 52
  differential association theory 47
  drift theory 52
  neutralisation theories 51–2
  social disorganisation theory 46–7
  status frustration 49
  see also youth crime
denunciation 99
determinism 41, 173
deterrence 100, 173
deviance 7, 173
deviancy amplification
    76, 79, 173
dictionary publications 134
differential association theory
    47–8, 109, 112, 173
differential opportunity theory
    50–1, 174
discrimination, running themes 14
'discuss' questions 164–5
divine power 17–18, 19
'doing masculinity' 96–7
domestic violence 120–1
drift theory 52, 174
drug use
  example essay points 161–2
  'victimless crime' debate 120
Du Cane, Sir Edmund 102
Durkheim, Emile 44, 48

economic issues
  right realism 57
  running themes 15
elite engineered approach, moral
    panics 82
empirical research 24–5
empirical validity, evaluating 131
'enlightenment' 20
epistemology 27–30, 174
escapes from prison 102, 103
essay writing tips 140–9
  balanced writing 142–3
  clarity 148
  conclusions 148
  critical approach 142
  evidence 145–6
  example questions 141, 142–3, 144
  introductions 147
  key concepts 141
  quotations 146–7
  structure 143–5
  topic selection 145
  tributary principle 140–1
essentialism 96
ethics 30–1
  secondary research and data 71
ethnographic research 27, 174
  status frustration 49
eugenics 37
evaluation
  criteria 130–2
  exam questions 152, 166–7
evidence
  crime statistics and data 68
  empirical research 24–5
  essay writing 145–6
  running themes 14
exam tips 155–68
  critical approach 163
  flight/fight/freeze response 161
  name dropping 160
  nerves 155–6
  parts analysis 163
  'politician's answer' 161
  practical details 158–9
  question spotting 162–3
  revision links 160
  time management 156–8
  wandering thoughts 159–60
Eysenck, Hans 38–9

falsifiable theories 131
Farrington, David 174
fear of crime
  media 77
  youth crime 85
Felson, Marcus 60–1, 174
feminist criminology 93–7, 174
  domestic violence 120–1
  liberal feminism 93
  masculinities 95–7
  radical feminism 93–4
  socialist feminism 94
  themes 45
  traditional criminology contrast 96
  victim surveys 72–3
Ferrell, Jeff 63, 175
feudal system 18
fictional crime 78, 82
flight/fight/freeze response 161
folk devils 79–80, 175
Foucault, Michel 20, 98, 175
fox-hunting, example essay plan 158
freewill 21–2, 35, 52, 175
functionalism 44

gang studies 49
Gaol Act 101
Garland, David 103–4, 175
gender *see* sex and gender
genes 40
genocide 115
geographical factors, crime
    definitions 7
Gladstone Committee 102
globalisation 114
glossary 170–81
goals of society 48, 51
Goffman, Erving 175
Goode, E. 81–2
Gottfredson, M. 53
governmentality 175
grassroots model (moral panics) 81

Hall, Stuart 81
hanging 18
health and safety breaches 111
hegemonic masculinity 92, 95, 176
Herrnstein, Richard J. 40
hidden crime 176
hierarchical systems (memory aids) 153

Hirschi, Travis 52–3, 176
Hobbs, Dick 176
Holford Committee 101
Home Office 68–70
homosexuality, crime definitions 6
Hood, Roger 176
Howard, Michael 58, 102, 122
hulks 101
human rights violations 10–11
hypotheses 26

ideology
    carceral punishment 104
    running themes 15
impact (crime stories) 78
imprisonment *see* prisons
    and imprisonment
incapacitation 100, 176
independent study 137–8
industrialisation 20, 104
inequality
    feminist perspectives 45
    running themes 14
institutional racism 45
integrationist criminology 78–9
intention to harm 22
interactionism 53–4
interest groups 9
interpretivist epistemology 28, 121
introductions (essays) 147
investment-group approach, moral
    panics 82
involvement bonds 53
Islington Crime Survey 67

Jones, Trevor 67
journal publications 66
journalist accounts 64–5
justice/justice system
    application of theory 131–2
    critical victimology 122
    feminist perspectives 45
    media impact 78
    peacemaking criminology 62
    running themes 15

Katz, Jack 63, 176
knowledge
    epistemological approaches 29
    power relationship 98

labelling theory 53–4
    criticisms 59
    media 78–9
    stereotyping 54
    victims of crime 119–20
Lange, Johannes 37
law, classical criminology 22
Lawrence, Stephen 119
learned behaviour 47–8
lectures
    making the most of 132–6
    notes 133–4
left idealism 44
left realism 58–60
    right realism contrast 166
    victim surveys 72
    victimology 121
legalistic position 8
legitimacy, prisons 106
Lemert, Edwin 53–4, 177
liberal feminism 93
life imprisonment, example essay
    points 142–3
local crime surveys 72
location method (memory aids) 153
logical consistency, evaluating 130
Lombroso, Cesare 36–7, 41, 94, 177
London Underground bombings 113

McKay, Henry D. 46
MacLean, Brian 67
Martinson, Robert 108
Marxist theory 9–10, 44–5
masculinities
    'doing masculinity' 96–7
    feminist criminology 95–7
    hegemonic masculinity 92, 95
    status frustration 49
Mathiesen, Thomas 177
Matza, David 51–2, 177
media 75–83
    coverage of crime 76–7
    deviancy amplification 79
    fear of crime 77
    moral panics 79–82
    news values 77–8
    positive representations 82
memory aids 152–4
men *see* masculinities
Merton, Robert 48, 177

Messerschmidt, James 49, 92, 96–7
Michael, J. 8
Michalowski, R. 10
Mill, John Stuart 19
mind maps 153–4
mnemonics 152–4
Mods and Rockers 80
monarchy 18, 19
moral panics 177
    contemporary examples 76
    media 79–83, 177
    youth crime 85
morality 19, 81, 132
Mubarek, Zahid 103
mugging, moral panics 81
murder
    classical criminology 22
    early victimology 119
    life imprisonment pros and
        cons 142–3
    serial murder 144–5
Murray, Charles 58, 177
myths 37, 95

name dropping 160
'name and shame' campaigns 83
National Offender Management Service
    (NOM) 103
neo-classical criminology *see*
    right realism
neo-conservative criminology *see*
    right realism
neo-Marxism 44
nerves (exams) 155–6
neutralisation theories 51–2
new deviancy theory 53–4
new journalism 65
news value (crime stories) 77
newspapers 64, 73, 76–7, 134
NOM *see* National Offender
    Management Service
notes
    lectures 133–4
    note-taking strategies 135–6
    organising 150–1
    revision 150
notifiable offences 69

occupational crime 111
offender accounts 64–5

official statistics 50, 68–71
Ohlin, Lloyd 50
oppression, women 93–4
organisational crime 111, 112, 178
organised crime 113, 178
origins of criminology 16–23
orthodox accounts, prison crisis 105
overt research 30

paedophilia
    crime definitions 6
    moral panics 80, 82–3
Panopticon 17, 178
Park, Robert E. 46
parsimony, evaluating 131
parts analysis (exam questions) 163
past exam papers 151
patriarchy 45, 122
peacemaking criminology 61–2
Pearson, Geoffrey 85
peg system (memory aids) 153
penal welfarism 102
penology 98–108
    see also prisons; punishment
Pepinsky, Harold 61–2
personality 38–40
police
    evaluating effectiveness 145
    recorded crime 69
    square of crime 59
political issues
    crime statistics and data 74
    criminological research 31–2
    realist criminology 56
    running themes 15
'politician's answer' (exam
    questions) 161
popular culture 78
positive media representations 82
positivism 34–5, 178
    aetiology 170
    classicism contrast 35
    quantitative research methods 26
positivist epistemology 28
positivist victimology 118
power
    conflict theories 44
    crime definitions 7
    divine power 17–18, 19
    Foucault's discourse 98

power *cont.*
　Marxist theory 10
　organised crime 113
　running themes 14
　victimology 117
primary research and data 25, 68
'Prison Works' speech (Michael
　　Howard) 102, 122
prisons and imprisonment
　example essay points 151–2
　future 107
　history 101–3
　life imprisonment 142–3
　positive media representations 82
　prison crisis 104–8
　right realist approaches 58
　young people's experiences 88–9
　see also penology
professional crime 112–13
psychological approaches 38–41
punishment
　Beccaria's challenge 19–21
　capital system 18–19
　corporal punishment 18, 104, 164
　death penalty 18, 20, 104
　example essay plan 141
　feudal system 18
　historical phases 103–4
　purposes 99–100
　responses 22
punitivism 104

qualitative research methods 26–7, 178
quantitative research methods 26, 178
question spotting 162–3
Quetelet, Adolphe 67, 74, 178
Quinney, Richard 10, 61–2
quotations (essay writing) 146–7

race, running themes 14
racial discrimination 45
radical accounts, prison crisis 105–6
radical criminology 44
radical feminism 93–4
radical non-intervention 87–8
radical pluralist accounts, prison
　　crisis 106
Radzinowicz, Leon 65
rape, early victimology 119
re-offending 88

realism 56–60, 179
reality, epistemological approaches 29
recidivism 179
recorded crime 68–9
rehabilitation 100
Reiner, Robert 179
reintegrative shaming 117–18, 123
relative deprivation 60
relaxation techniques 156
repeat victimisation 90
reported crime 69
representation of crime
　media 82
　running themes 15
research methods 24–33
　access 31
　combined methods 27
　epistemology 27–30
　ethics 30–1
　political issues 31–2
　primary and secondary research 25
　qualitative research 26–7
　quantitative research 26
　running themes 14, 24
restorative justice 62, 118, 122–3
retributivism 100
revision hints and tips 149–55
　exam links 160
　group revision 154
　mnemonics 152–4
　notes 150–1
　past papers 151
rhymes (memory aids) 154
right realism 57–8
　left realism contrast 166
　prison effectiveness 105
　victimology 122
ruling class 9–10, 20
running themes 14–15

Saunders, C. 63
Schur, Edwin M. 84, 87–8, 120
Schwendinger, Herman and
　　Julia 10–11
scope, evaluating 130
secondary research and data 25, 68
secondary victimisation 121
self-control 53
self-esteem 49
self-government 58

self-report studies 50–1
  limitations 72, 73
Sellin, Thorsten 8–9
seminars, making the most of 136–9
sensationalism 83
serial murder, example essay
    structure 144
serious crime 108–16
sex crimes, feminist victim
    surveys 73
sex and gender 91–7
  definitions 92
  female criminality 94–5
  feminist criminology 45, 93–4
  masculinities 95–7
  running themes 14
shaming 83, 117–18, 123
Shaw, Clifford R. 46
situational crime prevention 60
Smart, Carol 179
social constructions 11
  Felson's critique 61
  gender 92
social contract theory 22
social disorganisation theory
    46–7, 179
social exclusion 60, 121
social harm 10
social learning 179
social theory 179
  study skills 129–32
socialist feminism 94
sociological theories 42–55
  conflict theories 8–9, 44–5, 112
  consensus theories 44
  control theory 52–3, 111, 172
  differential association 47–8,
    109, 112, 173
  differential opportunity 50–1, 174
  drift 52, 174
  labelling, interactionism and new
    deviation 53–4
  neutralisation 51–2
  social disorganisation 46–7, 179
  status frustration 49
  strain 48–9, 130, 179
  see also feminist criminology
spirituality 17–18
square of crime 59, 121

stalking, crime definitions 6
statistics and data 66–75
  clear-up rates 69–70
  'dark figure' 69, 71–3, 173
  official statistics 50, 68–71
  political issues 73–4
  problems 73
  recorded crime 68–9
  victim surveys 67, 71–3
  youth crime 86
status frustration 49
strain theory 48–9, 130, 179
Strangeways Riot 102
structuring essays 143–5
study skills 127–68
subcultural studies 180
  British research 87
  differential opportunity
    theory 50
  status frustration 49
surveys 67, 71–3
Sutherland, Edwin Harding 10, 47,
    108–9, 112, 180
Sykes, Gresham 51–2
symbolic function, imprisonment 99
symbolic interactionism 53–4

tabloid newspapers 64
Tappan, Paul 10
Taylor, Ian 180
technical terms, mastering 134–5
Tennenbaum, F. 53–4
terrorism 113
testability, evaluating 131
time management, exams 156–8
top down clarity (essays) 148
topic selection (essays) 145
traditional criminology 96
  see also classical criminology
transferable skills 138
trans-national crime 114
transportation 18
'treatment' approach
  biological criminology 38, 41
  historical phases of punishment 104
  Martinson's critique 102
  purpose 100
tributary principle (essay
    writing) 140–1

underclass 58
Union Carbide Company (Bhopal) explosion 111
unreported crime 69
usefulness, evaluating 131–2
utilitarianism 19

validity, evaluating 131
value free perspectives 6, 28, 31
verstehen 63
victim-blaming 118–19, 121
victim surveys 67, 71–3
victimless crime 120
victimology 117–25
    critical victimology 122
    early victimology 118–19
    feminist criminology 120–1
    labelling 119–20
    left realism 121
    restorative justice 122–4
    right realism 122
    victimless crime 119–20
    young people 89–90
visualisation 153
vocabulary, developing 134
Vold, George 9
Von Hentig, Hans 119

Waddington, P.A.J. 81
war crimes 115

welfarism 102, 104
'what works' approach 61, 102
white collar crime 109–12, 180
    social harm definition 10
    victim surveys 72
Wilkins, Leslie 76, 79
Wilson, David 181
Wilson, James Q. 40, 57–8, 111–12, 116, 181
Wolfgang, M. 119
women
    capital system 18
    criminality 94–5
    feminist perspectives 45
    see also feminist criminology
Wormwood Scrubs investigation (1998) 103

Young, Jock 59, 67, 180
youth crime 84–91
    American research 86–7
    British research 87
    prison experiences 88–9
    radical non-intervention 87–8
    subcultural studies 87
    see also delinquency

zero tolerance 58
zone of transition 47